edexcel
advancing learning, changing lives

Construction

BTEC Level 1 Introductory
Certificate and Diploma

Sue Meredith **John Cartwright** **Gary Cumiskey**

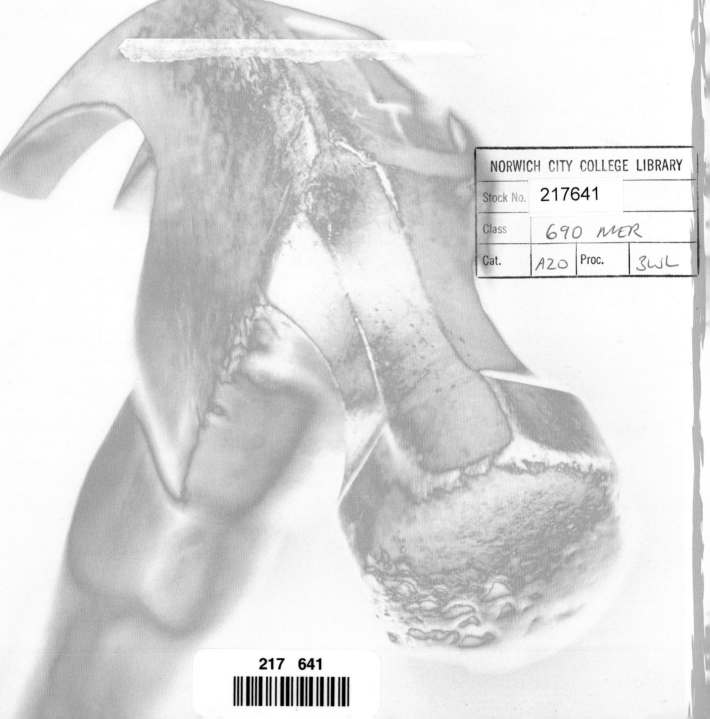

Published by
Edexcel Limited
One90 High Holborn
London
WC1V 7BH

www.edexcel.org.uk

Distributed by
Pearson Education Limited
Edinburgh Gate
Harlow
Essex
CM20 2JE

www.longman.co.uk

©Edexcel Limited 2007

First published 2007
10 9 8 7 6 5 4 3 2 1
British Library Cataloguing in Publication Data is available from the British Library on request

10-digit ISBN 1-84690-065-0
13-digit ISBN 978-1-84690-065-2

Commissioned by Jenni Johns
Design and publishing services by Steve Moulds of DSM Partnership
Cover image courtesy of (top) Constructionphotography.com, (bottom) JupiterImages
Project edited by Julia Bruce
Picture research by Thelma Gilbert
Index by Joan Dearnley
Printed in Spain by Mateu Cromo, S.A. Pinto (Madrid)

Acknowledgements
Alamy pp 24 (Mediacolor); 25 (Jochen Tack); 81 (Mediacolor); 111 (David Green); 126 (Jenny Matthews); 153 (Mediacolor); 158t (Photofusion); 193 (Photofusion). **Constructionphotography.com** pp 6; 14; 16; 19; 29; 37; 56; 57; 95; 112; 132b; 142; 146; 149r; 151; 155; 158b; 159t; 165; 168; 176; 185; 199b; 206. **Corbis** pp 71; 99; 194. **Empics** p 17. **Photos.com** pp 13; 45; 62; 77; 107; 217. **Rex Features** p 51. **Roger Scruton** pp 11; 21; 33; 132t; 140; 143; 152; 157; 159m,b; 160; 201b; 202; 207; 208.

The publishers wish to thank **Screwfix Direct** (www.screwfix.com) and **Stanley Tools** for supplying photographs of tools.

Websites
Please note: at the time of writing, all the web addresses given in this book were correct and contained active pages.

Contents

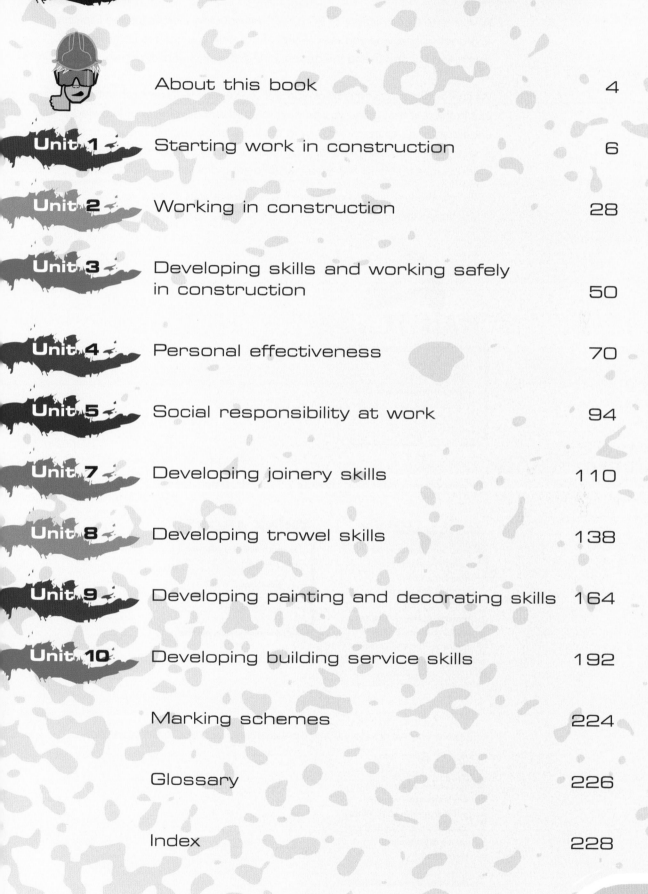

About this book

Welcome to *Construction: BTEC Level 1 Introductory Certificate and Diploma*. This book will provide you with all the information you need to complete the core units (1, 2 and 3) and the option units 4, 5, 7, 8, 9 and 10 of the qualification.

When you first look at this book you will see various features both in the margins and in the text that guide you on how to build and develop your knowledge and understanding. Apart from covering the knowledge you will require, this book also provides you with many opportunities to collect evidence for your portfolio. The activities that help with your portfolio are indicated in various ways:

✳ Follow the weblinks to get more information about an area you are interested in.

NAIL IT

Find out more about apprenticeships by visiting the apprenticeships website:
http://www.apprenticeships.org.uk

✳ Fix your understanding by doing these short activities.

DRILL DOWN

Find out what sort of abrasives painters and decorators use. Information can be obtained from manufacturers or you can research these on the internet. Place your list in your portfolio.

TH!NK ABOUT

In which activities do you use your:

✳ **gross motor skills?**

✳ **fine-motor skills?**

✳ Ensure you work safely by using these hints and tips in the workplace.

SAFE✝Y TIP

Never use white spirit or any solvent to remove paint from the skin. White spirit is an irritant and can cause dry skin and dermatitis.

* Short definitions of important construction terms are given both within the text and, sometimes, also as a margin note. The word or term in the text is shown in **bold**.

Carpentry – is normally concerned with structural woodwork.

Joinery – is concerned with furniture making and small-scale wood constructions.

* Activities that provide practical experience. This can be recorded in your portfolio.

TRy THIS

Practice interviews

Ask your supervisor or trainer to help you to role-play practice interviews for the two jobs you have applied for. Make sure that you take the time to prepare for the role-play interviews according to the advice earlier in this section.

* Activities that make you think about your course and any practical work experience. You can make a short record of this for your portfolio.

WHAT WOULD YOU DO?

Suppose you want to become a carpenter or joiner when you leave school. Try to answer the following;

* Who do you need to speak to for guidance and information?

* What questions would you need to ask them?

* Activities to complete and record in your portfolio.

EVIDENCe

Matching your strengths to particular jobs

Using the information you have gathered so far about your work skills and preferences, find at least two job descriptions from newspapers or the internet which would suit your skills.

To help you understand technical and other terms used in this book, definitions are listed in a glossary starting on page 226. This includes the terms that have been defined in the margin notes, and more besides. Glossary terms are given in bold the first time they occur in the book. This page reference is also listed against each term in the glossary itself to make it easy to refer back to it and see it used in context.

We hope you enjoy using this book in your studies, and we wish you the very best for your course and future career in Construction.

Starting work in construction

At the end of this unit you should be able to...

* identify a range of different types of jobs in the construction sector

* match different construction jobs to the skills and qualities needed

* identify the different types of organisation operating in the construction sector

* select and describe an organisation where you may like to work

* list the lifestyle factors that affect jobs in the construction sector.

1

Unit overview

This unit describes the fascinating variety of work available in the construction and built-environment industry. Specialist jobs range from architecture, involving design and drawing, through to the skilled craft of creating the designed structure. Each specialist job requires a unique set of skills and training, and for every job in the construction industry a very strong commitment to health and safety is vital. You need to consider which path may suit you best.

You will also have choices about the type of organisation you could work in. Most of the organisations operating in the construction industry are small companies, specialising in a particular type of work – for example a renovation company or a plumbing company. On the other hand, there are some very large organisations in the construction industry employing hundreds of staff with different types of qualifications.

In the following pages, you will have the opportunity to start investigating the different types of work and workplace available to you in this career and to consider which types of work match your own abilities and preferences.

Many different types of job are available in the construction industry.

Different types of jobs

In this section you will learn about...

* the different types of professional jobs in the construction industry

* the different types of craft jobs in the construction industry.

Jobs vary according to the skill, knowledge and personal qualities required to perform the work tasks involved, the amount of responsibility expected, the amount of training and education required and opportunities for advancement. Jobs also vary in terms of the number of hours worked (full-time, part-time, casual), and this relates to the amount of job security.

Job categories

Jobs in the construction sector can be:

* full-time or part-time

* employed or self-employed

* permanent, temporary or casual.

For example, a person may be employed as:

* a casual, part-time, unskilled operative – this is quite an insecure job, requiring the minimum level of training

* a full-time, permanent, supervisory technician – this would be a much more secure job, with a higher level of responsibility – and more pay!

Full-time and part-time work

A person employed full-time can normally expect to be working for an average of 48 hours a week. If you are under 18, a full-time position should not exceed eight hours a day and 40 hours per week. The general cut-off between jobs defined as full-time and those defined as part-time is 30 hours per week. Some people may work part-time in two different jobs.

Employed or self-employed?

When you work for an organisation, the financial and administrative aspects of your employment are managed by the company, including insurance, wages and tax. The company may also provide tools and equipment, arrange for regular maintenance of equipment and provide equipment and clothing for health and safety. When you work for yourself, either as a sole trader or in your own small business, you have to take responsibility for all these matters – this is required by law. Being self-employed requires good business skills as well as the skills of your chosen profession. You also have to find work for yourself, for example by advertising. The income of the business can be very different from the amount you end up being able to pay yourself in wages.

WHAT WOULD YOU DO?

Choose one of the following 'what if' activities to complete. Spend some time working independently and researching your topic, then discuss your ideas with a partner or in a group.

What if you had two part-time jobs?

Imagine that you had two part-time jobs, then answer the following questions:

1. Would the jobs you chose involve the same or different types of work?

2. Which two jobs would you choose?

3. What are the benefits of having two different jobs?

4. What are the drawbacks of having two different jobs?

Discuss the benefits and drawbacks of having two different jobs with a partner or in a small group.

Take notes of the discussion and prepare a summary of the key points to present to the class.

What if you had the opportunity to set up your own business?

1. What business would you set up?

2. Where would you get advice and help?

3. What are the benefits of having your own business?

4. What are the drawbacks of having your own business?

Discuss the benefits and drawbacks of having your own business with a partner or in a small group.

Take notes of the discussion and prepare a summary of the key points to present to the class.

NAIL IT

Find out more about employment status and your rights by visiting the Trades Union Congress (TUC) and Worksmart websites:

http://www.tuc.org.uk/tuc/youngpeople.pdf

http://www.worksmart.org.uk/

Permanent, temporary and casual work

When you are employed by an organisation, your job security depends on whether the position is permanent, temporary or casual. A permanent position is the most secure, and the employer must have a good reason for ending your employment. They should let you know if the job is going to end in good time so that you can find another one – this is called 'giving notice'. Temporary employment is usually very short-term and people are often employed as 'temps' to cover for the absence of permanent staff. Casual employment may last for a few weeks or months, and usually covers a busy season, when extra staff are needed for a given time. Quite often, people are employed on a casual or temporary basis before being offered a full-time position.

Career streams – professional, craft and operative

In the construction sector, jobs tend to fall into three categories:

* professional and technologist – those that generally require a degree or similar level of qualification
* craft – skilled trades that require some level of qualification
* operative – semi-skilled or unskilled jobs that often don't require any qualification.

Professionals and technologists include:

* architects
* construction technologists
* engineers
* surveyors
* managers.

Craft jobs include:

* bricklaying
* carpentry and joinery
* plumbing
* painting and decorating
* electrical installation.

Operative jobs include:

* scaffolding
* labouring.

A skilled operative may have some training and several years of building and construction experience. An unskilled operative would be just starting training, or working as a general labourer.

During a career in the construction industry, you might span all three of these categories. Figure 1.1 shows just one possible career path.

1999	2001	2004	2006	2012	2015
unskilled operator	skilled operator	qualified carpenter	Business manager	Degree in structural engineering	Project manager large new residential estate

Figure 1.1 Career paths continue for your lifetime at work.

Job roles in professional and technologist areas

Most of the following job roles require a degree or equivalent level qualification. They may also require further professional qualifications to be taken to progress your career.

⚑ Architects

Architects create designs for new buildings and for the conservation and restoration of existing buildings, particularly those of historical interest. Architects are also involved in ensuring that the actual construction work complies with the design. This involves consulting and negotiating with everyone involved in the project. Architects must be imaginative and creative, be able to draw in three dimensions and use computer modelling systems. They also need excellent communication and interpersonal skills. Training for this job takes seven years of combined education and work experience in an architect's office.

⚑ Architectural technicians and technologists

An architectural technician works out the methods and techniques to be used for drawing up designs. This includes preparing technical information, ensuring statutory regulations and quality standards are met and organising project information. A person with Higher National Certificate or Diploma qualifications may work as an architectural technician while studying to become a technologist.

Architectural technologists investigate technical architectural problems and design solutions, which include researching and selecting the best materials for the job. They also provide technical support, negotiate with planning and building authorities and supervise the architectural elements of construction work. Architectural technologists may work with an architect or by themselves, producing detailed designs and specifications which comply with all legislative and regulatory requirements. Training is usually done while working, by attending day-release courses for a degree in Architectural Technology.

⚑ Building surveyors

Building surveyors are employed by organisations such as local authorities, construction and engineering firms and building conservation bodies to

NAIL IT

Find out more about architecture as a career by visiting the Alec website:
http://www.alec.co.uk/free-career-assessment/architect-career-information.htm

Being able to transfer your vision to paper is essential for an architect.

NAIL IT

Find out more about architectural technology by visiting the website of the Chartered Institute of Architectural Technologists:
http://www.biat.org.uk/index.jsp
http://www.biat.org.uk/_uploads/about/CareersHandbook2005.pdf

supervise whole building projects. Building surveyors provide advice about structural matters and the design, construction, maintenance, repair, renovation and conservation of all types of building. The training for this work would start on the job with a surveying firm and involve working towards NVQ/SVQ in Property Management or Building Control.

Civil engineers

Civil engineers deal with the engineering processes involved in the planning, construction and maintenance of fixed structures or public works. Most civil engineering today deals with power plants, bridges, roads, railways, buildings, water supply, irrigation, the natural environment, sewers, flood control, transportation and traffic. A civil engineer may be a:

* **consulting civil engineer** who plans, manages, designs and supervises construction projects
* **contracting civil engineer** who ensures that the actual construction work is completed to plans, time and budget.

A Bachelor of Science (BSc) or Bachelor of Engineering (BEng) degree in civil or structural engineering is the usual entry level to this career, although in some organisations it is possible to start as a trainee technician on an Advanced Modern Apprenticeship. You could then gain experience on the job, become registered as an engineering technician and work towards becoming an incorporated or chartered civil engineer.

Structural engineers

Structural engineers are responsible for making sure that a construction can withstand all the pressures and strains, such as weight, in all the relevant structural supports. A degree in structural or civil engineering is required, but you can start working towards becoming a structural engineer with a Higher National Diploma (HND).

Engineering apprenticeships

It is also possible to start work in construction engineering through apprenticeships in areas such as building services engineering and engineering.

Managers and supervisors

As you get more experienced in the construction industry you may take on supervisory or project management responsibilities in addition to the work related to your specific skill. Construction managers usually have a degree in building, building studies, construction engineering management, building technology or building management.

Find out more about apprenticeships by visiting the apprenticeships website: http://www.apprenticeships.org.uk

Wood occupations – skills concerned with carpentry and joinery.

Trowel occupations – skills concerned with bricklaying and plastering.

Job roles in craft and operative

Entry into most jobs in the crafts sector of the construction industry is also through apprenticeships. You'll find more about this at the apprenticeships website. Those available in the construction industry are:

* construction (craft) apprenticeship including **wood occupations**, masonry and **trowel occupations**

* electrical and electronic servicing apprenticeship

* mechanical engineering services: plumbing apprenticeship.

Bricklaying

Bricklayers use materials such as bricks, blocks, lintels, stone and mortar to build and maintain structures including walls, chimney stacks and archways. Tools used include trowels and spirit levels. The work involves following plans to set out the dimensions of the structure, gathering the correct materials, mixing mortar and then laying the courses of bricks or blocks according to the design. A bricklayer must be very fit, committed to safe working methods and prepared to work outside in all weathers and in noisy, dirty, wet environments. The training required for qualified bricklayers is NVQ/SVQ in Trowel Occupations. This is usually completed at work with some block or day-release training at a college.

NAI**L IT**

Find out more about trowel occupations by visiting the Learn Direct website:

http://www.learndirect-advice.co.uk/helpwithyour career/jobprofiles/ category11/

case study

Sam was looking for a job that suited his preference for doing something with his hands and that involved craftmanship, that is, good control and attention to detail. He decided that a career in trowel occupations would be the best option and found work with a company where it was also possible to complete NVQ Level 2 in Trowel Occupations – Bricklaying on the job, with part-time study. Sam went on to complete NVQ Level 3 in Trowel Occupations – Bricklaying, and an Ordinary National Certificate (ONC) in Building and Construction. He is now self-employed as a qualified bricklayer.

Questions and activities

1. What is the minimum length of time that it would have taken Sam to complete all the training?

2. How much 'off-the-job' training is involved in:

   NVQ Level 2

   NVQ Level 3

   ONC?

3. What other skills and knowledge does Sam need to be able to operate as a self-employed bricklayer?

4. Using the internet, and possibly interviews with self-employed people within your own network, find out the following:

   * What courses are available for people wanting to be self-employed?

   * Which organisations or government departments offer support and advice to self-employed people?

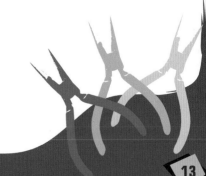

Stonemasonry

Stonemasons work with materials such as sandstone, slate, marble or granite to produce cladding, window frames and archways, and to repair historical buildings. The stone is cut with hand and power tools, mortared in place and finished according to plans and specifications. The training required is towards NVQ/SVQ in Stonemasonry and is usually provided on the job, as an apprentice with some block or day release at college. Stonemasonry can be very specialised in renovation work.

Carpentry and joinery

The work performed by carpenters and joiners involves creating and installing structures, fixtures and fittings from timber for residential and commercial projects. The work may involve installing roof trusses and partitions or making floorboards, cupboards, doors and window frames. A carpenter and joiner must be fit and prepared to work in all weathers, and at heights, and be committed to safe work methods. The work may be noisy and dusty. The training required for carpenters and joiners is NVQ/SVQ in Wood Occupations, with options to specialise in bench work, site work, shopfitting or timber frame erection.

Roofing

Roofers build and repair roofs and may work in roof slating and tiling, flat roof work with felt and mastic asphalt, roof sheeting and cladding, lead sheeting or even thatching. A roofer must be fit and prepared to work in all weathers and at heights and be committed to safe working methods. The training for this work varies depending on the type of roofing speciality, and includes NVQ/SVQ in Roofing Occupations, Mastic Asphalt, Roof Sheeting and Cladding and Applied Waterproof Membranes.

> **Carpentry** – normally concerned with structural woodwork.
>
> **Joinery** – normally concerned with furniture making and small-scale wood constructions.

Thatching is a traditional roofing skill still used today.

Wall and floor tiling

Wall and floor tilers apply ceramic, stone and man-made tiles to walls and floors. They use cutters to cut tiles to size and shape, adhesives to secure them in place and grout to finish between the tiles. Tiles may be placed in intricate patterns and mosaics according to the architect's or designer's plans and specifications. The training for this work is NVQ/SVQ in Wall and Floor Tiling.

Plastering

There are three types of plastering, solid, fibrous and dry-lining. Solid plasterers use mixtures of sand and cement and pebble-dash to finish off, and often provide a texture to, walls and floors – both inside and outside. Fibrous plasterers use fibrous materials to make mouldings, such as ceiling roses and cornices. Dry-lining plasterers use plasterboard to make internal partitions. The training for this work is NVQ/SVQ in Plastering.

TRY THIS

Try out some practical work experience and informational interviewing (see page 36) about different jobs.

Practical experience

Make arrangements with your teacher/trainer to spend time on work experience at different types of workplace, or in on-site workshops, if these are available.

Note down what skills and knowledge you learned and how much you enjoyed each experience. Keep this information for future reference.

Painting and decorating

Painters and decorators prepare surfaces such as walls, floors, doors and fixtures. They apply finishes such as paint, varnish or wallpaper, using brushes, rollers and paint-spraying equipment. Some artistic creativity is involved when assisting clients in the selection of colours, patterns and finishes. Paint and varnish products do produce fumes, so painters and decorators must wear appropriate PPE. Painters and decorators should also be able to work at heights and be committed to safe working practices. The training for a qualified painter and decorator is NVQ/SVQ in Decorative Finishing and Industrial Painting Occupations.

General construction operative

Also known as building operatives, groundworkers or labourers, general construction operatives perform most of the labour-intensive and less skilled work on a building site. This work may include digging holes and trenches, setting up scaffolding, concreting and preparing materials for the craft workers. The training for this work is NVQ/SVQ in Construction and Civil Engineering Services (Construction Operations) Levels 1 and 2.

Electrical installation

Electricians install, inspect and test wiring and equipment in residential and commercial buildings. The work could involve stripping out old wiring and replacing it, or installing a completely new system following plans and specifications. This includes installing cabling and wiring and then connecting the wiring to sockets, switches and fittings. *An electrician must be extremely safety-conscious.* The training for an electrician working in the construction sector is Electrotechnical NVQ (2356), Electrotechnical Services: Electrical Installation (Building & Structures) or Electrical Maintenance.

DRILL DOWN

Electricians have to do a lot of maths in their training and learn some important mathematical laws. Ohm's law is one. It can be summarised as $V=IR$. Can you find out what V, I and R stand for? If you enjoy maths, you might consider becoming an electrician.

A plumber can specialise in work on domestic properties.

Plumbing

Plumbers work with water, gas and ventilation systems involving pipes. This includes hot and cold water supply, leadwork, sanitation and waste disposal systems, central heating systems, roofing and drainpipes and gas supply systems. Plumbing work includes installing new systems according to a designed plan and specification, and also the repair and maintenance of existing systems. Plumbers must be fit and prepared to work at heights and in all weather conditions. They must be committed to safe working methods. Training for this occupation is City & Guilds (6089) NVQ Level 2 and 3 in Mechanical Engineering Services (MES): Plumbing and City & Guilds (6129) Technical Certificate Level 2 Basic Plumbing Skills and Level 3 Plumbing Studies.

Informational interviews

Informational interviews involve you talking to an experienced person in a particular career, to find out about the work they do. Choose the areas of construction work that you would like to find out more about. With the help of your teacher or trainer, identify a person in each of these areas who would be willing to spend half an hour showing you the work and answering your questions. Prepare your questions well before attending the informational interview. Take notes and prepare a summary of the information you obtained.

EVIDENCE

Find out the details of five different jobs – at least two from the professional area and two from the craft and operative area.

Conduct your research by:

* interviewing people working in these jobs – refer to informational interviews information

* visiting career advisory services

* studying material available on the relevant websites – some of these are listed in the margin notes of this section.

Different types of organisation

In this section you will learn about...

* organisations operating in the construction industry

* the scope and nature of organisations in the construction industry.

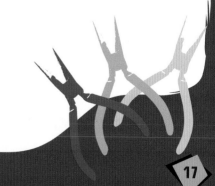

Construction is the largest industry in the UK, employing over two million people. There are many different organisations, both large and small, involved in construction and operating at local, regional and national levels. These include not only operational companies but also regulatory organisations, professional organisations and trade unions. Construction organisations are concerned with the whole range of activities from domestic maintenance to major public construction projects, such as the building of the new Wembley Stadium.

The new Wembley Stadium is one of the largest construction projects in the country.

Organisations operating in the construction industry

There are many different organisations involved in the construction industry operating at local, regional and national level. They include:

* national and local government – whose main role is to enact and enforce legislation

* statutory bodies – organisations set up by government to manage certain aspects of industry management, for example training

* industry organisations – bodies with members drawn from the industry whose main role is to represent the views and interests of the members to government and to the public

* trade unions – member organisations that protect the rights of workers

* commercial companies – profit-making organisations, both large and small, which employ construction staff

* charitable institutions – for instance the Lighthouse Club (see p20).

Government and statutory organisations

National government departments

* **Department of Trade and Industry (DTI)** – responsible for trade, business, employees, consumers, science and energy. The DTI's Construction Sector Unit (CSU) covers policy and regulations (such as improving payment practices), industry performance (such as health and safety and training), sustainability and innovation.

* **Health and Safety Executive and Commission (HSE/HSC)** – responsible for enforcing the regulations governing health and safety to protect the health and safety of people at work, and making sure that risks in the workplace are controlled effectively.

Local government

* **Local municipal councils** – may have bye-law regulations and building inspectors and surveyors who monitor and control construction activities.

* **Local authorities** – required by the HSC to take responsibility on their behalf for the enforcement of health and safety regulations in the local area.

Statutory bodies

* **Construction Skills** – the Sector Skills Council for construction covering construction crafts, such as carpentry and joinery and bricklaying, and professions such as architecture and building surveying. The organisation works towards ensuring that the 88,000 new recruits required each year receive the training and qualifications required by the industry.

* **Summit Skills** – the Sector Skills Council for building services engineering. It deals with issues of recruitment and training for work in providing electrical power, heating, air conditioning, ventilation, refrigeration and plumbing in all types of building.

Industry associations

* **Construction Industry Council (CIC)** – represents over 25,000 construction firms on issues connected with construction.

* **Construction Industry Research and Information Association (CIRIA)** – aims to improve the quality, efficiency, cost-effectiveness and safety of the built environment.

Trade unions

Trade unions are organisations that look after the interests of their members – workers in various industry sectors. To join a trade union you have to work in a

NAIL IT

Find out more about the DTI Health and Safety Executive by visiting the websites:
http://www.hse.gov.uk/
http://www.dti.gov.uk/
sectors/construction/
index.html

NAIL IT

Find out more about trade unions by visiting the websites:
UCATT:
http://www.ucatt.org.uk/
GMB:
http://www.gmb.org.uk/
TGWU:
http://www.tgwu.org.uk/

relevant job and pay a membership fee. Benefits of membership include access to help and advice, and national representation of your industry sector to employers and government. There are several trade union organisations that have an interest in the construction industry.

* **Trades Union Congress (TUC)** – this an umbrella organisation for all trade unions, and campaigns on issues common to all work areas.

* **Union of Construction, Allied Trades and Technicians (UCATT)** – this is a specialist union with over 120,000 construction worker members.

* **GMB** – Britain's general union, with 600,000 members working in all different sectors of the economy.

* **Transport and General Workers Union (TGWU)** – another general union with 800,000 members.

Commercial companies

There are over 170,000 construction firms in the UK. Only five per cent, that is less than 9000, of these companies employ more than ten people. There are three main types of business in the UK:

* **Public limited companies (plcs)** – companies with a share value of over £55,000. They may have an unlimited number of shareholders and sell shares to the general public. Most of the largest construction companies, employing thousands of staff, are public limited companies.

* **Private firms (limited companies)** – have between two and 50 shares. No shares may be sold without the agreement of other shareholders. Many of these companies are family-owned businesses and are usually small- to medium-sized.

* **Sole traders** – businesses owned by one person. They tend to be small, and may only involve the business owner themselves.

> ## DRILL DOWN
> See if you can find out why Britain's general union is called the GMB. The answer is somewhere on its website.

There are thousands of small businesses and sole traders in the construction industry.

DRILL DOWN

See if you can find any other charitable organisations linked to the construction industry. Are they national or local? What do they aim to do?

Charitable institutions

Two charities with a particular interest in the construction industry are:

* **CRASH** – the construction and property industry charity for the homeless that works to improve the accommodation provided for homeless people. http://www.crash.org.uk/

* **The Lighthouse Club** – a charity with a benevolent fund used by the trustees to provide assistance to construction workers and their families who need financial support due to accident or illness. http://www.lighthouseclub.org/

Scope of operations

A construction company may concentrate its advertising and activities in a local area, or tender for large national or even international projects, depending on the size of the company and the vision and mission of the organisation's leaders.

International operations

Specialist organisations may be involved in projects worldwide: for example, a small architectural firm may specialise in the design of sport and leisure centres. Very large companies will also tender for construction contracts in other countries that are especially suited to their experience, for example building hospitals.

National operations

National operations could cover the whole of each of the countries making up the UK – England, Northern Ireland, Scotland and Wales – or the whole of the UK. You would have to be prepared to live away from home for periods to work for a company like this.

Regional operations

Construction companies with the capacity to tender for larger contracts would extend their operations to a whole region, such as the Highlands of Scotland or the southeast of England. A region would usually cover about six counties.

Local operations

A company confining operations to the local area would probably advertise and conduct their work within one county, for example Worcestershire. A very small company may just confine their work to one large town and the outlying small villages. Most of these companies would be small, with between one and ten employees.

Size

The majority of construction companies are small, employing between one and ten people, but the larger companies employ more staff.

Large contractors

The largest construction companies operating in the UK include:

* Tarmac

* Carillion

* Alfred McAlpine

* AMEC

* Balfour Beatty

* Costain Group

* John Laing

* Kier Group

* Mowlem

* Taylor Woodrow.

A large-scale construction project

NAIL IT

Find out more about large companies operating in the construction industry by visiting the Corporate Watch website: http://archive.corporate watch.org/profiles/ construction/construction2. htm#overview

Small and medium enterprises

There are over 250 000 construction companies in the UK. The majority of these companies employ fewer than ten people each.

* 70 000 companies employ 1 person

* 55 000 companies employ 2–3 people

* 25 000 companies employ 4–7 people

* 10 000 companies employ 8–13 people

* 6000 companies employ 14–24 people

* 4000 companies employ 25–60 people

* 1500 companies employ 61–300 people

* 150 companies employ 301–600 people

* 75 companies employ 601–2000 people

* 60 companies employ over 2000 people.

Nature of operation

A lot of firms will specialise in a particular area of construction. Some of these specialisms will depend on size. A sole trader, for instance, is unlikely to specialise in large public works. Some typical areas of operation include:

* large public works, such as hospitals, prisons and schools

* infrastructure, such as bridges

* speculative house-building, that is large residential developments or estates

* newbuild, conversion and adaptation, that is individual house-building or renovation

* maintenance and repair of existing structures

* manufacture and supply of components.

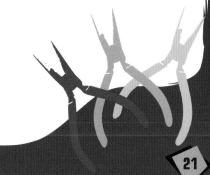

EVIDENCE

Look in the local business telephone directory or use the internet or local papers to find examples of the different types of business operating in the construction industry in your region. Make sure you include at least one example of the following types of organisation:

* government bodies (national and local)

* statutory bodies

* public limited companies

* private firms

* sole traders

* large organisations

* small to medium organisations

* charitable institutions.

Select three different types of construction company. Base your selection on the size of the company, the scope of the company's operation and the nature of the work undertaken. Choose companies that you may like to work for.

For example:

* a large company specialising in building hospitals all over the world

* a small plumbing firm specialising in roofing, and working only in the local area

* an architectural firm specialising in historical restoration work in the regional area.

When you have identified your three companies, answer the following questions:

1. How many staff are employed in the company?

2. What job roles do the staff have?

3. What major projects has the company been involved in over the last two years?

4. Would you like to work for this company? Why? In which job role?

Lifestyle and job choice

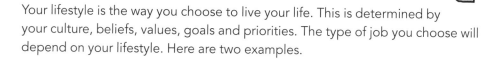

In this section you will learn about...

✴ **how to select a job that suits your lifestyle**

✴ **work patterns.**

Your lifestyle is the way you choose to live your life. This is determined by your culture, beliefs, values, goals and priorities. The type of job you choose will depend on your lifestyle. Here are two examples.

You may wish to devote most of your time and energy to your construction career and very quickly get to the top of your craft or profession, earn the best wages and gain status within your family and community.

You may wish to balance the time you spend on your construction career with other important aspects of your life, for instance starting a family or pursuing other ambitions such as sport or music.

Lifestyle

It is important to match your job to the choices you make in the rest of your life.

Before deciding on a particular career in the construction industry, or a type of company, consider how the following possible requirements could affect your lifestyle:

✴ early start

✴ occasional long hours

✴ working outside in all weathers

✴ living away from home

✴ prolonged strenuous physical activity

✴ repetitive work

✴ working indoors

✴ wearing personal protective equipment

✴ working near dust or fumes

✴ noise and vibrations from machinery

✴ working at heights

✴ working in confined spaces

✴ changing project sites

✴ changing project teams.

◆ Effect of lifestyle on job choice

If you have regular commitments to interests and activities outside your work, such as spiritual organisations, sports or family commitments, you may have to limit your job choices. Some jobs in construction may require you to work away from home, work shifts or work overtime for significant periods.

◆ Individual ambitions and aspirations

We spend a lot of our adult life working so it is important to take time to find out what you enjoy, what you're good at and which job suits you. People are happiest in jobs that they are confident and skilled in, that feel more like fun than work and that suit their personality and their likes and dislikes. It is important to decide how skilled you wish to become, and whether you want to work for someone else or be your own boss. How much training are you prepared to do? Apart from just keeping up with changes and innovations in the industry, how highly qualified do you intend to become?

◆ The benefits of work

Everyone needs to earn enough to pay the rent or mortgage, eat and drink, keep themselves in clothes and shoes, pay for transport and go out occasionally – but most people want much more from their work. For many people work is something they take pride in and feel fulfilled by. The workplace is somewhere they make lifelong friends with common interests.

case study

Craig runs his own small business, building house extensions. When he is busy, he sometimes advertises for casual staff to help out. Craig gets frustrated when people who seemed enthusiastic about the job at the interview turn up late for work, take long breaks and don't do the job properly. 'Some people just haven't got the right motivation for a career in construction', says Craig. 'I'm looking for people who are prepared to work efficiently and effectively and to work as part of a team. If you're working for me, you need to be a perfectionist in your skill area. This career is not for the faint-hearted – you have to be prepared to work hard, keep faith in your ability to succeed and keep learning from more experienced workers. Construction is a vocation, not just a job.'

Questions and activities

1. What could happen to Craig's business and his reputation if the casual workers he employs are unreliable and careless?

2. If you went for an interview for a casual job with Craig, how would you convince him that you were committed to your career and wouldn't let him down?

Job choice

Work in the construction sector can offer many opportunities to explore your own skills and abilities. It can even give you the chance to travel and see the world. You should also gain great work satisfaction from your chosen career. Your work is essential, creative, practical and highly visible. Construction workers fulfil one of the greatest of human needs – the need for shelter.

Skills in demand

Skilled construction workers are in great demand and there is a global shortage in many crafts and professions. Construction workers may be employed by large companies to contribute to significant projects worldwide. Smaller companies often work on projects in different regional areas. Even if your work is based in a local town, you may find yourself working on different types of project in different localities.

Work patterns

In selecting your ideal job, you need to consider the work patterns required of you. Are you, for instance, prepared to:

* work away from home?

   This may be for weeks at a time, and may allow travelling home on weekends, depending on how far away the job is and whether the expected completion date requires weekend work.

* work abroad?

   Large companies will tender for projects worldwide – you could have the opportunity to work in Europe or further afield, for example China or India.

You could be working abroad if you apply for a job with the right company!

* work long hours or on weekends?

Building projects run to tight timeframes, and there are many things that can upset the best plans for finishing on time. Companies have to pay penalties or fines for late completion of projects, so if construction is running late, you will often be asked to work long hours and at weekends. Weekend work may also be required when conducting maintenance or repairs on business premises.

* work flexitime?

This means that your average number of hours per week stays the same, and you get the same pay, but your working hours may vary. For example one day you start at 6.00 am and finish at 6.00 pm, the next day you may start at 8.00 am and finish at 4.00 pm. Flexitime may be used to make sure that, for example, the carpenters are not wasting time waiting around for the plumbers to finish a task before they can start work.

* start work at six in the morning?

Although there are limits on the times that you can start work that causes noise, it is possible that some projects will have very early start times. There's no guarantee you will be able to pick and choose which projects you work on. Early starts mean making sure that you have had enough sleep to be fit and alert and ready to start work when required.

* spend more than an hour travelling to work?

The headquarters of the building firm may be close to home, but each project will be in a different location. Are you prepared to set off at 5.00 am to get to work on time?

Stress levels

Stress has a very negative effect on your health in the long term. In the short term, stress can affect your ability to concentrate and your hand-to-eye coordination. Stress may arise from:

* personal and family problems

* being allocated to work tasks beyond your level of skill

* being teased and bullied in the workplace

* having tight deadlines and trying to work too fast.

If you are feeling stressed you must take steps to deal with it, as the lack of concentration and coordination could result in serious accidents or incidents. Talk to your supervisor, union representative or a family member.

Physical requirements of work

Many of the on-site jobs in the construction industry require high levels of health and fitness. In addition, you may need the ability to work at heights or in small spaces. You also need to be able to use heavy and noisy equipment and tolerate dust, dirt and extremes of temperature. Off-site work in design, supply of materials or administration is not so physically demanding, but some site visits may still be required.

WHAT WOULD YOU DO?

What if you could choose the ideal job?

1. Make up a brief job description for your ideal job

or

2. Research jobs that really appeal to you in the newspaper or on the internet.

Make sure that the information includes hours of work, travelling required, type of work and, if possible, career prospects.

Explain why you have chosen this job, and how it suits your lifestyle.

EVIDENCE

In addition to your set work and study hours, do you intend to commit any extra time to pursuing your career? Have you done any of the following?

* Stopped at a construction site to observe the work being done?

* Searched the internet for information about construction work, not related to your current study requirements, but just out of interest?

* Spoken to experienced construction industry workers about careers, job methods or other topics?

1. Choose one of the activities above. If you have already done all of them in your spare time, choose the one you spent the least time on, or the one you found most worthwhile. Before starting the activity, note down what you intend to do and what you hope to find out.

2. Complete a summary of your findings.

Working in construction

At the end of this unit you should be able to...

* describe the terms and conditions of different jobs in the construction sector

* explain why companies provide induction courses, and describe the induction and training procedures in one particular organisation

* explain why it is important to monitor work performance, and describe the procedures used to monitor performance in one particular organisation.

2

Unit overview

This unit aims to show you what it's like being at work. It covers the day-to-day realities of being a construction worker. In addition to the chosen skills of the work, a construction worker must be flexible, committed, safety-conscious and a team player.

One of the key factors for successful construction companies is making sure that projects are completed on time. Workers are sometimes asked to exceed the usual expectations of the job, for example by working long hours. Contributing willingly in this way helps the company to succeed and thrive – and ultimately makes your career more secure. You will also find that your contribution will usually be noticed and rewarded.

Each construction workplace will have:

* **terms and conditions** of employment, which set out the contractual agreement about the hours and status of the job, the pay rate and any entitlements, such as holidays or tool money

* an **induction** into the company, including getting to know the key people, finding your way around and an introduction to company systems for such things as time sheets and wage payments

* **training** for the tasks defined in your job description and the associated procedures that you have to follow

* **company procedures** for monitoring your work performance and progress.

There is a lot to find out about when you start working in construction.

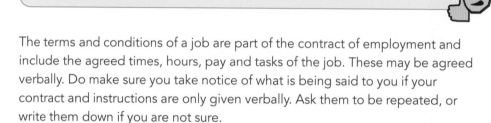

Terms and conditions

In this section you will learn about...

* starting work

* working patterns

* pay and conditions

* health, safety and welfare.

The terms and conditions of a job are part of the contract of employment and include the agreed times, hours, pay and tasks of the job. These may be agreed verbally. Do make sure you take notice of what is being said to you if your contract and instructions are only given verbally. Ask them to be repeated, or write them down if you are not sure.

Starting employment

When you are first employed you should be given information about how the workplace operates and what the job involves. In a workplace with a culture of respect, all your questions should be answered. The employer should be concerned that you are happy with the work, your colleagues and supervisors.

◪ *Respect for People* initiative

This programme started in 2000, after a construction-industry working party reported back to the government on ways to improve relationships between employers and employees, and between construction organisations and the general public. *Respect for People* involves improving workers' satisfaction and the workplace culture so that skilled workers will want to work for and stay with the company. A series of **toolkits** was developed to assist businesses in improving people management and achieving industry standards. The toolkits include strategies for working on:

* equality and diversity in the workplace

* working environment

* health

* safety

* career development and lifelong learning

* worker satisfaction.

◪ Contract of employment

As soon as you agree to work for an employer – and they agree to hire you – you have a **contract of employment**. This does not have to be written down to be binding, but you should receive a written statement of the **terms and conditions** of your employment within two months of starting work. The contract of employment cannot override any legal entitlements that you have,

> **Toolkit** – in this context, toolkits are sets of guideline documents drawn up to help companies develop and maintain good working relationships with their employees.

for example the right to the minimum wage. Most contracts would have, as a minimum, details of:

* your job title

* hours of work, including maximum hours of overtime

* normal wages, overtime rate and bonuses

* holiday entitlement, usually four weeks minimum

* sick pay

* pension schemes

* length of notice required – this applies to:

    – the employer – if you are no longer required

    – to you – if you no longer wish to work for the company

* grievance, dismissal and disciplinary procedures.

The contract of employment may refer to other material, such as the **staff handbook**, for up-to-date information on entitlements. This means that the employer can change the information in the staff handbook instead of re-drafting everyone's contract of employment. You need to make sure that you keep up to date with these changes.

NAIL IT

Find out more about contracts of employment by visiting the Adviceguide website:
www.adviceguide.org.uk/index/life/employment/contracts_of_employment.htm

Staff handbook

The staff handbook contains detailed information about the company and may cover the following items:

* the vision, mission and goals of the company

* the organisational structure

* the general rights and responsibilities of both employers and employees

* key company policies, procedures and programmes.

The handbook may be given out and explained during the induction programme. The staff handbook is usually updated and improved through feedback from new employees – so any questions you have about the company and your rights and responsibilities may be answered in this book. The updates may also include changes in the general terms of employment or changes in pay and bonuses.

Public notices

You should always be notified of any changes in company policies or procedures that may affect your terms and conditions of employment. This notification may be a change in the staff handbook, or a public notice on the company website, in a newsletter or newspaper, or on the staff notice board. It is important that you know where company information is published and that you access these locations to keep up to date. Certain changes affecting you may be communicated by a personal letter as well as, or instead of, a public notice.

NAIL IT

You can find out more about TUPE on the DTI website
www.dti.gov.uk/employment/trade-union-rights/tupe/page16289.html

Transfer of Undertakings (TUPE)

If your company is taken over by another company, then the TUPE regulations ensure that the terms and conditions of your employment are kept the same under the new company.

❑ Flexibility

Most construction companies will build some flexibility into contracts of employment to allow for the changes to working hours and conditions that are sometimes required to ensure a project is finished. There may also be some flexibility written into your contract regarding the type of work that you are required to do. If there is a rush to get a job finished, for instance, the employer may need your help in a different area for a while. Being flexible is a key attribute for all employees, showing a willingness to adapt and contribute to a team effort. If you never want to work overtime or flexitime, or outside of your chosen skill area, you need to make sure that these requirements are not included in your contract.

❑ Short-term employment patterns

A pattern of short-term employment means having several different jobs in a year, spending anything from a week to a couple of months in each. This is a pattern of work that some casual construction operatives may have, but it can show a lack of commitment and possibly a lack of skills – otherwise companies would want to keep them on. It is much better to research the type of work that you will enjoy and the type of company you want to work for, so that when you start a job, the chances are you will be happy to stay there for at least two years.

❑ Self-employment

A self-employed person has the responsibility for all aspects of their business including:

* keeping accounts

* paying taxes

* making sure they have the right insurance

* advertising for customers

* estimating and quoting for jobs

* buying all the tools and materials for a job.

It may be great to be your own boss, but you really have two jobs when you are self-employed – running the business and doing the work.

In some cases an employer may take you on as a self-employed worker or sub-contractor. However, you are not self-employed when:

* you only do work for one employer

* the employer is responsible for marketing to customers and finding work

* the employer asks you to do the work

* you do not have to provide a 'quote' for doing the job

* if you cannot go into work, the employer asks someone else to do the work – it is not up to you to find someone to take your place

* the employer tells you how the work should be done

* the employer pays you regularly, not at the end of the job, and you do not have to provide an invoice in order to get paid

* the employer provides the materials and some, or all, of the tools for the job.

NAIL IT

Find out more about being self-employed by visiting the Small Business website:
www.smallbusinessbible.org/

Pay

It is important to know how often you are paid, and how much you will receive after deductions, so that you can budget your money. If you are paid monthly, you will need to be very organised about how you spend your wages. There are regulations covering pay rates and you should be aware of your minimum entitlements, not just for your base wage, but also for any special allowances you are entitled to receive.

Method of payment

Wages are usually calculated on an hourly rate and paid weekly, fortnightly or monthly. Some companies issue cheques and others will pay wages directly into your bank account; very few organisations pay cash. If you are paid cash in hand, then you are probably not legally employed and not paying tax. **Salaried** staff have an annual amount of pay that is split into monthly or fortnightly amounts.

> **Salary** – your pay is agreed as an annual amount and paid in equal amounts throughout the year, usually monthly or fortnightly.
>
> **Wages** – your pay is calculated on an hourly, daily or weekly rate, or on a piece-work rate, and you are paid weekly, fortnightly or monthly according to the amount of time worked, or amount of work done, in that period.

Being paid cash in hand may mean you are not legally employed.

Working rule agreements

A working rule agreement sets out the standards of pay and entitlements for a particular industry. In 2005, the Construction Industry Joint Council (CIJC) issued a working rule agreement, detailing minimum amounts for:

* entitlements to basic and additional rates of pay

* daily fare and travel allowances

* storage of tools – employer's maximum liability

* loss of clothing – employer's maximum liability

* subsistence allowance

* sick pay

* benefit schemes.

NAIL IT

Find out more about the working rule agreement for the construction sector by visiting the UCATT website:
www.ucatt.org.uk/Indnews_pri1.htm

Rates of pay and conditions

In the public sector, the Joint Negotiating Committee (JNC), for local authority craft and associated employees, negotiates pay and conditions for local

DRILL DOWN

When you are paid by an employer, certain amounts will be deducted from your pay. Can you find out what three of these deductions might be? What is your pay called before deductions are made? What is it called after the deductions have been taken?

PAYE – Pay As You Earn. Deductions, such as national insurance, income tax and company pension scheme contributions are taken out of your pay before you receive it.

government craft workers in England and Wales. The JNC produces the 'red book' agreement, which is a national agreement on pay and conditions of service.

Deductions

Certain amounts of money may be deducted from your gross pay under **PAYE** arrangements. Tax and national insurance are deducted by the employer and paid to the government on your behalf. You may also have amounts deducted from your pay, and automatically paid in to the correct account, for any of the following:

* union dues

* contributions to a retirement pension scheme

* additional health insurance scheme.

Work patterns

Work patterns refer to the way your working hours are arranged over the week, month or year. For example, a shift work pattern might be early shift for a week, then afternoon shift for a week, then late shift for a week. In the construction industry you may have different work patterns in the summer and winter, due to the hours of daylight. In midwinter the sun doesn't rise until about 8.00 am and it's dark by 4.00 pm, but in summer it's light at 6.00 am and still light at 9.00 pm.

Hours of work

The hours that you are contracted to work should average out to 40 hours a week or less. Some contracts specify the number of hours per month or year to allow for flexible daily or weekly work hours. This may result in irregular work hours instead of the same start and finish time every day and the same number of hours per week. In these circumstances, unless other arrangements are made, the weekly pay packet could vary.

Irregular work patterns

The planning of large construction jobs is complex. The aim is to move teams across the project one after the other – one task has to be finished before another can start. For example, carpenters and bricklayers will be working on the structure of the building before the electricians and plumbers add the services, and the painters and decorators will be one of the last teams through the project. If one team is held up, then the plans for starting all the other teams have to be adjusted. This is why the company will be asking you to be flexible about work hours. If everything goes according to plan, all well and good, but if things go 'pear-shaped' some changes in work hours and days may be required. Irregular work patterns may include:

* shift systems

* early starts

* late finishes

* flexitime

* days off

* annual leave.

Holidays

You are entitled to holidays, and the number of days should be specified in your contract. Some of your holiday entitlements are explained below.

◪ Annual leave

In the UK you are entitled to a minimum of four weeks of annual leave; if you work full-time this would be equal to 20 working days. If you work part-time, then you get 'pro-rata' holidays, that is, proportional to the amount of days that you work.

So if you work three days a week, four weeks' holiday would be equal to 12 working days. Some employers may give extra annual leave as an employee benefit.

You should be aware that the four weeks of annual leave can include public holidays (bank holidays) – see below.

◪ Special leave

Special leave is time off work that you are entitled to take, but may not be paid for. Your job should be kept open for you to return to at the end of the leave period. Special leave includes:

* time off to have and /or look after a new-born child or adopted child, or any child you are responsible for under the age of six.
  These are covered by:

  - maternity leave

  - paternity leave

  - adoption leave

  - parental leave.

* emergency leave. This includes:

  - time off for looking after sick children

  - time off for funerals and recovery from the death of a person close to you (also called compassionate leave)

  - time off for jury service

  - time off for study or training

  - time off for medical appointments.

◪ Public holidays

Most employers allow employees to take public holidays as an additional holiday – but there are no laws in the UK to force employers to do this. Some employers can, and do, ask employees to work on public holidays or to take annual leave.

The UK has the smallest number or public holidays (eight) of all the countries in the EU.

Benefits

In addition to your pay in actual cash, there are other items and services offered by some employers free, or at reduced expense. For self-employed workers, these benefits are within your own control.

Tool allowance

Some employers pay a tool allowance to workers to ensure that the tools they are using are kept well maintained, and replaced when worn or damaged.

Bonuses

Bonuses are extra payments, such as a 'Christmas bonus' traditionally paid by some employers, and by others if the business is doing really well. Some employers may pay an incentive bonus for finishing a project on time and up to all the relevant quality standards.

Meals on duty

Many construction companies have a canteen or catering service provided by the company where the cost of meals is subsidised – that is, the employer makes a contribution to the cost of providing the meals, so the food is much cheaper than usual.

Use of facilities

Some organisations have leisure facilities, such as a social club or a gym, available for the use of employees. This might be owned by the company or it might provide free or subsidised membership of local facilities.

Working away from home subsistence allowance

A subsistence allowance to cover room rental and meals is paid when an employee has to work away from home. This is usually a daily allowance.

Season ticket loans

Some companies will give employees free or low-interest loans so that they can save money on annual season tickets for public transport travel to and from work. This may only be for one particular means of travel, such as a warrant for a rail season ticket but not for a coach season ticket.

◖ Free clothes and personal protective equipment (PPE)

Construction companies should supply hard hats, goggles, earplugs, gloves and any other specialist PPE. Some companies also provide company uniforms or overalls and jackets, and may subsidise the purchase of protective footwear.

◖ Pensions

When you retire from work, you are entitled to a weekly amount of money from the government. This is generally known as 'the old age pension'. This amount may not be enough to support your usual lifestyle. For this reason, many people pay a percentage of money from their wages into a pension fund run by the company they work for, or into a private pension fund, to be used when they retire. If you join a company pension scheme, the money is deducted from your wages before the tax is taken out, and your company also makes a contribution.

◖ Skills development and training

Any training or skills development you receive at work is also a benefit, as you would have to pay to do this if you were not employed. The more training and development you do receive at work, the better it is for your career.

> **NAIL IT**
>
> **The Pension Service website provides information about occupational pensions. Find out more by visiting the website:**
> www.thepensionservice.gov.uk/

case study

Khalid works as a maintenance joiner for a large construction company employing over 50 people. In addition to Khalid's regular pay, the company provides:

* a pension scheme
* a private health insurance scheme
* a company shares scheme
* a company van
* clothing allowance
* tool allowance.

Khalid thinks the conditions of employment are very good and has stayed with the company for 20 years.

Questions and activities

1. Do you think it's important to belong to a company pension scheme? What are the benefits?

2. What are the benefits of owning shares in the company you work for?

3. Think about the benefits of having a company van. How much do you think this is worth in real cash per week?

4. Research the amounts paid by a selection of construction companies for the tool and clothing allowances.

   Try and choose some small and large companies to research. Is there a difference between them regarding the amount they pay?

Safety, health and welfare

There are many hazards in construction industry environments. It is therefore particularly important to remember that both the employer and employee have responsibilities for ensuring safety, health and welfare.

Personal responsibility

Every employee has a responsibility to:

* follow company procedures and work instructions

* use the personal protective clothing and equipment required for each task

* work safely, by using prescribed, safe work methods

* use, store and maintain tools and equipment correctly

* be aware of hazards and risks and take recommended measures to avoid these.

Personal protective equipment (PPE)

The types of personal protective equipment you may be required to use include:

* head and face protection, such as:

    - a hard hat to protect the head against falling objects

    - a broad-brimmed hat to prevent sunburn

* eye protection, such as:

    - a welding visor, protecting the eyes from bright light and sparks

    - goggles, to protect the eyes from dust

* ear protection, such as:

    - noise-blocking ear muffs, protecting the ears from very loud noise – these are sometimes attached to hard hats

    - ear plugs – disposable plugs protecting the ear from medium-level noise

* respiratory protection, such as:

    - a dust mask – to prevent breathing in light dust

    - a respirator with a built-in filter – provides full cover and protection from heavy dust

    - a positive air respirator – provides full protection from the surrounding air and is used in situations where the air has toxic contaminants, such as asbestos dust

* hand protection, such as:

    - rubber gloves, protecting from long-term exposure to water

    - heat-resistant gloves, for working with hot metal

    - chemical-resistant gloves, for protection from acid burns

* foot protection, such as:

    - steel toe-capped boots to protect the foot from being crushed and permanently damaged if a heavy weight falls on it

* whole body protection, such as:

  – sturdy overalls, offering some protection from scratches

  – sunscreen, to protect from UV rays which can cause skin cancer.

Commonly used PPE –
hard hat, goggles, dust
mask, steel toe-capped
boots, ear defenders.

First aid

First aid is the immediate simple assistance that can be given to the victim of an accident by a person who is not medically trained. It is intended to:

* keep the person alive until medical aid arrives

* prevent the injuries from getting worse

* help the person to recover from the injury.

You should be told where to find the first aid box and who is the trained first aid person in your area of the workplace.

EVIDENCE

1. Compare the terms and conditions of at least three jobs in different sectors of the construction industry, for example:

   – painter and decorator

   – plumber

   – electrician.

2. Choose one type of job from question 1 and find out whether the terms and conditions differ in, for example:

   – a large private company employing over 50 people

   – a medium-sized company employing about 20 people

   – a small company employing less than five people

   – an owner-operated company.

3. Collect some samples of contracts of employment. Using these as a reference, create a contract of employment that you would use for your employees if you ran a small business employing five or more people.

Induction and training

In this section you will learn about...

* what happens when you start work
* different types of work training
* apprenticeships.

Induction is the process of introducing new employees to the workplace and to their job. It helps them to become familiar with some of the basic information required to perform well as a company employee.

Training might include classroom sessions, workshop sessions, observation of skilled staff and practising of new workplace skills.

Starting work

Induction is one of the most important aspects of starting work. In the induction programmes and associated information you should receive everything that you need to know about the company and the job. In many organisations you will also receive induction training on each new project and at each new site. There is a lot of information to absorb, and much of this should be reinforced at a later date in ongoing training or other forms of information distribution. Induction training may take the form of:

* self-paced online or multimedia programs
* workplace tours and introductions
* classroom sessions with guest speakers
* demonstrations, for example, of safety procedures
* handouts and booklets.

Induction training should cover topics such as:

* the structure of the organisation
* the structure of the relevant department and names of staff
* introductions to key staff, such as your supervisor or team leader, manager, health and safety representative, union representative and human resources personnel
* your team members and their responsibilities
* statutory regulations that apply to your work
* the expected standards of respectful behaviour and interpersonal relations
* the expected standard of dress and any specific clothes, uniform and personal protective equipment, such as boots with steel toe-caps, that you are required to wear in the workplace

* basic health and safety training, including safe lifting and handling of equipment

* Provision and Use of Workplace Equipment Regulations (PUWER) requirements

* procedures to be followed in the case of fire

* first-aid arrangements

* accident reporting procedure

* procedures for the use of dangerous substances and COSHH regulations

* procedures to follow in the case of absence due to sickness or bereavement

* procedures for arranging annual leave.

Training

Training is education in specific vocational skill areas that continues after you have left school. People working in various industries undergo entry-level training to start off in a job, and then build careers by undertaking higher-level training.

Skills development

Skills development involves practising your skills in different projects and scenarios, maybe using different materials and methods. If you do this you will build up your expertise and confidence in your chosen profession. It is important to take on challenges, to try new methods and to ask more experienced people to show you their methods and techniques.

Further education and training

You can continue formal training and professional development through workplace programmes and college courses. These will help progress your career and give you recognised qualifications.

Construction Skills Certification Scheme (CSCS)

The CSCS card scheme started ten years ago and is managed by CITB Construction Skills. There are now over 800 000 card-holders in the industry. The card lists the relevant training completed and certifies that a person is competent in their job and is health and safety-conscious. The card also acts as an identity card.

Apprenticeships

As an apprentice, you learn while you are employed, so you receive wages, work at your job and spend some time in training programmes either at work or at college. In the construction industry, the following apprenticeships are available:

* building services engineering

* construction (craft)

* electrical and electronic servicing

* engineering

* mechanical engineering services: plumbing.

DRILL DOWN

What can you find out about COSHH? What does it stand for? How do you think COSHH might affect you in the workplace?

NAIL IT

Find out more about the Construction Skills Certification Scheme by visiting the website: www.cscs.uk.com/

NAIL IT

For more information visit the apprenticeships website at www.apprenticeships.org.uk

On-site Assessment and Training (OSAT)

OSAT is a process for recognising the skills and experience of construction workers who may not have completed formal training. The applicant is assessed against the requirements for recognised qualifications, and if successful in all the relevant subjects qualifies for a CSCS card.

Updating knowledge and skills

It is important to keep in touch with what is happening in the construction industry. Most importantly, you should check whether there are any changes in laws and regulations that affect your work. You can also develop your skills and keep up with changing work methods and technology by attending workshops, seminars and conferences. You will also make useful contacts and build your own professional network, which could help with future employment options.

Other ways of keeping up to date and developing your skills and knowledge include:

* subscribing to relevant industry magazines

* joining an industry association.

TRY THIS

Find out what industry associations exist for the sectors of the industry you are most interested to work in. Check out their websites. Quite a few have special membership rates for students or apprentices. Find out how much it would cost you to join, and decide what you personally might get out of membership. Industry associations are good sources of career information too. See what career advice you can get for the sector of your choice. Write a report of your findings.

Procedures used to monitor performance

In this section you will learn about...

* **performance review and appraisal**

* **assessment**

* **quality standards**

* **qualifications**

* **work procedures**

* **disciplinary and termination procedures.**

Performance monitoring involves checking to ensure that the induction and training provided, combined with the skills and efforts of the staff, produce the required outcomes in terms of the quality of work and productivity – that is how much work gets done in a particular timeframe.

Most companies will check to make sure that the time, money and effort spent on induction and training is as effective as possible. If work quality and productivity are not meeting expectations, then the company will ask questions, such as:

* Are we selecting the right sort of people for the job?

* Are we providing enough training?

* Is the training of good quality?

* Are we providing enough support for new staff?

Individual performance review and appraisal

Periodic performance appraisal is one way to assess how a person is progressing on the job, and to find out how that person would like to develop their skills and their career.

A performance appraisal will:

* evaluate individual performance and progress

* set goals for individual achievement

* ensure appropriate training and development is planned

* confirm the person's role in the organisation, and outline prospects for improvement.

When starting a job, performance appraisals may be held quite frequently, for example, after the first month, then after two or three more months, then after six months. Most performance appraisals continue annually after the first year. Performance appraisals may be managed and/or conducted by the human resources, training or personnel department of a large organisation, or by a consulting firm specialising in performance appraisal. The people participating would include the individual concerned, the person's team leader or immediate supervisor, and/or the section manager.

The process may include:

* self-evaluation of skills and abilities, strengths and weaknesses

* supervisor's appraisal

* functionality tests

* completion of questionnaires

* discussion of results

* negotiation of training and development for the coming year

* preparation of a personal performance plan.

EVIDENCE

Choose one of the following two activities.

Induction

Review your own experience of induction training. This may have been:

* a group induction course for part-time workers in a large store (Saturday job)

* induction information given to students attending college part-time as part of completion of NVQs or similar training

* informal induction, at a part-time job or work experience placement, where you are shown round by an experienced worker and this person explains essential information to you.

Gather together any materials that you may have kept and use these to plan a short induction programme for new entrants to a workplace or organisation that you know quite well. List all the information and activities that you would include to prepare the new entrants for starting work.

Performance appraisal

Research methods used for performance appraisal by interviewing the human resources personnel in one selected company, and/or by conducting internet-based research. Consider the questions you want to ask before arranging and conducting the interview. Collect as much written information about the performance appraisal process as you can. After reviewing all the material, answer the following questions:

1. How does the employee benefit from individual performance appraisal?

2. How does the organisation benefit from performance appraisals?

3. What types of performance goals and targets are set?

4. How can the employee improve personal performance?

5. How can the organisation help the employee to improve their performance?

Assessment

In addition to performance appraisal, assessment of competency in particular skills and tasks will be held at various times, depending on the training you receive. You may be required to answer questions, for example about the hazards associated with a task. You may be given specific tasks or small projects to complete. Your work will then be assessed against the work instructions, specifications and quality standards for the job. You may be asked to complete a self-assessment, which can be compared to an assessment by a line manager and/or assessments by work colleagues.

Quality standards

There are international, European, national and organisational quality standards that may relate to your chosen field of work. Quality standards are codes of best practice that improve safety and efficiency. They are necessary to make sure that buildings are safe and that all the services and fittings work effectively and efficiently. Failure to work to established quality standards could result in building faults and serious incidents.

◗ Quality standards relevant to your job

You should be advised of any quality standards relating to your job as part of the induction procedures and initial training. The requirements of relevant quality standards are usually written into company procedures and work instructions in the same way as legal requirements.

Some examples of British Standards (BSI) that apply in the building and construction industry include:

* BS 5628-1:2005 Code of practice for the use of masonry.

* BS 7671:2001 Requirements for electrical installations.

* BS 7974:2001 Application of fire safety engineering principles to the design of buildings.

BSI also administer **ISO 9000** – a family of standards that can be applied across industries and provide a framework for quality management systems.

NAIL IT

Find out more about British Standards and ISO 9000 by visiting the website:
www.bsi-global.com/index.xalter

case study

Lou is an electrical installations inspector and tester. Lou says: 'This work requires patience and logical thinking patterns – you also have to be very careful to follow all the requirements of British Standard 7671'. In order to inspect and test electrical installations, Lou needs to use up-to-date equipment that meets the requirements of the standard. Lou adds: 'You need to understand the complexity of the job and apply safe isolation procedures to avoid electrical shock, electrocution and electrical burns'.

Questions and activities

1. In your own words, explain why it is important that construction work meets set standards.

2. List the standards that apply to the area of construction work that you are most interested in. You can find out by:
  - questioning skilled people
  - doing your own research on the internet.

3. Discuss the following with your colleagues, supervisor or teacher:
  - How do construction organisations make sure that standards are met in everyday work tasks?
  - What could happen if a project was completed, but on inspection, it was discovered that the building did not comply with all of the relevant standards?

◙ Construction Skills Certification Scheme (CSCS)

The CSCS card scheme contributes to quality processes as it certifies that construction employees are competent to perform their job tasks and are health and safety conscious.

◙ Apprenticeships

The apprenticeship system ensures that construction employees receive quality training that covers all essential standards and codes of practice. These are written into the training and assessment requirements for passing through the levels of the apprenticeship.

◙ National Occupational Standards

National Occupational Standards (NOS) describe the outcomes that can be expected from competent performance of a particular skill. Training and assessment guides and materials are then written to conform to the standard. This ensures that a person qualifying as a carpenter in one college, for example in Wales, has a similar level of skill and knowledge to a person qualifying from a college in the Highlands of Scotland, or in Cornwall. They cover all the main aspects of an occupation, including current best practice, the ability to adapt to future requirements and the knowledge and understanding that underpin competent performance.

The NOSs are used to plan and support individual and company development and to provide quality assurance.

◙ National Vocational Qualifications (NVQs)

National Vocational Qualifications (NVQs) are work-related, competence-based qualifications. They reflect the skills and knowledge needed to do a job effectively, and show that a candidate is competent in the area of work the NVQ represents.

NVQs are based on National Occupational Standards. These standards are statements of performance that describe what competent people in a particular occupation are expected to be able to do.

The trainee undertaking an NVQ must be assessed as competent before the qualification is awarded and the trainee moves to the next level.

The NVQ levels apply to workplace levels of responsibility as follows:

* **Level 1** – performs a range of routine and predictable work activities

* **Level 2** – performs a wide range of work activities; some tasks will be complex or non-routine and/or unsupervised; the person would often work as part of a team

* **Level 3** – performs a broad range of complex and non-routine work activities, taking responsibility for the work and often controlling or guiding others

* **Level 4** – performs a broad range of complex, technical or professional work activities, taking responsibility for a part of a project

* **Level 5** – takes responsibility for projects, including analysis, diagnosis, design, planning, execution and evaluation.

NAIL IT

Find out more about the National Occupational Standards by visiting the website:
www.standards.dfes.gov.uk/learningmentors/nos/

At each level, a specified number of units of training must be completed. For example: to achieve NVQ Level 3 Technical Design (Built Environment), you need to complete:

* U1053070 Confirm requirements for and prepare technical designs

* U1053071 Produce drawings and schedules

* U1053072 Provide technical information

* U1053073 Manage yourself and your working relationships

and select one of the following:

* U1053074 Contribute to contract tendering and cost control

* U1053075 Contribute to implementing project design

* U1053076 Contribute to implementing construction of the product

* U1053077 Observe and present physical survey data

* U1053078 Record the condition of property and installations.

Related Vocational Qualifications (RVQs)

These qualifications are also based on National Occupational Standards and are parallel in level to NVQs. Examples are technical certificates and City & Guilds qualifications.

Investors in People (IIP)

Investors in People is a standard for business and quality improvement through investment in the training and good management of people employed in the company. The standard is based on the principle that, in order for a business to do well, the people in the business must have the knowledge, skills and motivation to work effectively.

Client's specification

The quality standards set down by legislation and by the companies' own goals and policies may be very high, but these are the minimum level of standards that you will have to work to. The client you are working for may want the work completed to a much higher level. This will be described in detail in the specifications for the job.

NAIL IT

Find out more about Investors in People by visiting the website: www.iipuk.co.uk/IIP/Web/default.htm

The importance of quality standards

Quality standards are important as they ensure that:

* the company, the employees and the client have an agreed understanding of the quality of the finished project

* the finished project will be durable and safe

* all legislative and regulatory requirements are met

* the company improves its image and reputation and therefore gets more work – which means that the employees continue to have a job!

Ask your teacher, trainer or supervisor to set you a task, relevant to the construction sector in which you are interested, that involves completing work to a set quality standard. This should be a small project that can be completed in a relatively short time. The quality standard for the task may be:

* a British or European Standard

* organisational standard

* client specification of quality standard.

Study the requirements of the standard carefully before starting, and ask your trainer or supervisor to clarify anything that you do not completely understand.

Ask your supervisor, teacher or trainer to assess the quality of your work when you have completed the task. Discuss with your supervisor, teacher or trainer any suggestions for improving the quality of your work.

Other relevant workplace procedures

There are other workplace procedures that you need to understand and follow in order to do your job properly. They cover a variety of areas, such as security, safety and grievance procedures.

Security procedures

These relate to the safety of people, tools, equipment, materials and the structure of the projects – there will be workplace procedures for:

* making sure that property is stored correctly and locked up

* ensuring that everyone on-site or in the office is identified and strangers cannot cross into 'staff only' areas

* making sure that premises are secured, windows shut and doors locked.

Accident reporting

All workplace incidents and accidents must be reported so that the health and safety team or officer can work out how to prevent them from happening again. If you have an accident, or witness an accident, you will be required to complete an incident report form.

Grievance procedures

These cover any complaints you may have about the workplace, such as incorrect or poorly maintained tools and equipment, or being asked to do work that you are not qualified to do.

Disciplinary procedures

These procedures cover problems that the company has with your work attendance or performance, and involve a series of warnings about the behaviour and recommendations for improvement. Behaviour that would result in disciplinary procedures includes:

* taking sick leave without a doctor's certificate
* turning up for work late more than a couple of times
* unsafe behaviour
* bullying.

Termination procedures

These cover the methods of ending a contract of employment. This may occur for several reasons including:

* **redundancy** – the company not having enough work for all employees. The company is required to give you notice of redundancy, and in some cases may give you a redundancy payment. The size of this is normally related to your length of service with the company.

* **dismissal** – an employee's failure to respond to disciplinary procedures, or committing a very serious breach of procedures, may result in termination of employment. Dismissal is usually a last resort and, except in cases of gross misconduct, is normally preceded by a lengthy sequence of verbal and written warnings, eventual dismissal only occurring if these warnings are systematically breached or ignored.

* **job restructuring** – the company re-allocating work tasks and job roles so that some employees are no longer required. This can be related to redundancy.

* **resignation** – the employee no longer wishes to work for the company. This can be due to any number of factors including moving to a new job or new area, changing career, starting a family, setting up your own business and so on. You are required to give the company notice of your intention to leave. This notice period is normally set out in your terms and conditions of employment.

Retention

The minimum period of notice depends on the job retention period – the length of time you have worked for the company. Generally the notice period is one week if you have been with the company for less than two years, two weeks for two full years and an extra week for each extra year up to a maximum of 12 weeks.

Developing skills and working safely in construction

At the end of this unit you should be able to...

* identify construction work environments where there is a potential to cause harm, and to describe the risks and hazards

* identify construction materials that could cause harm

* identify the level and scope of your responsibility for the health and safety of yourself and others

* identify how and when to use different types of personal protective equipment

* identify where to find information on the control and safe use of hazardous materials

* describe the correct evacuation procedures for emergency situations

* describe the main objectives of first aid and the contents of a first aid box

3

Unit overview

Every worker in the construction industry must prioritise health and safety. In very broad terms, the health and safety objective of all construction workplaces is to be accident- and injury-free, to cause no damage to property and equipment, and to present no danger to the general public. The legal and organisational requirements for health and safety precautions and procedures must be very carefully applied to all preparation and work tasks. You need to be alert to the hazards and risks that may occur in different situations and be aware of the organisational requirements for dealing with these situations. For example, for most manual tasks there will be a requirement to wear specific types of personal protective equipment (PPE), such as a hard hat, goggles or protective gloves. In emergency situations, such as a fire, there will be a detailed set of procedures to follow.

There are many different hazards on a construction site – you need to be prepared and alert.

Safety helmets, protective footwear and high visibility jackets must be worn

Potential harm in the work place

In this section you will learn about...

* **accidents and how to avoid them**

* **tools and how to look after them**

* **hazards in the workplace**

* **hazards caused by construction materials.**

In the last 25 years, more than 2500 people have died from injuries received while working in construction. The most recent annual figure for deaths caused by accidents or injuries in the construction industry in the UK is about 70 per year. Many more people are permanently injured and unable to work.

Accidents

The types of accident that most frequently cause death and serious injury in the construction industry are:

* falls from a height, such as falling:
    - through a fragile roof
    - through a skylight
    - from a ladder
    - from a scaffold
* being hit with force, such as by:
    - moving plant, including excavators, lift trucks or dumpers
    - falling loads
    - falling equipment
    - being crushed by a collapsing structure.

NAIL IT

Find out more about accidents at:

www.hse.gov.uk/construction/index.htm

▶ Definition of an accident

An accident can be defined as:

> 'any unplanned event that results in injury or ill-health to people, or damages equipment, property or materials but where there was a risk of harm.'

The term 'accident' as applied to the workplace includes falls and slips; injuries caused by tools, equipment and materials; poisoning; and violence inflicted by others. It does not include deliberate, self-inflicted injuries, commuting incidents – that is incidents that occur on the way to or from work – illness or injury having a medical origin only, or occupational diseases.

An accident may be caused by:

* unsafe conditions, such as:
  - the presence of asbestos
  - incorrect scaffolding construction
* unsafe acts, such as:
  - failing to wear a hard hat on-site
  - incorrect storage or maintenance of tools and equipment.

Current accident-cause data

Up to 80 per cent of accidents are caused through human error. People make mistakes when they:

* do not have enough information or knowledge
* do not have the required skill or level of skill
* are tired and lack concentration
* are stressed or hurried.

In the construction industry, the majority of accidents are falls, slips and trips. These accidents result in over 1000 long-term injuries per year. The majority of them could be avoided if employers and employees paid more attention to keeping the workplace in good order, ensuring that:

* walkways and stairways are kept clear of obstacles and cables
* spills are cleaned up promptly and carefully
* everyone on-site is wearing appropriate footwear.

Tools and equipment

Using hand tools may seem easy, but quite serious injuries and disabilities, such as blindness, may be caused when construction workers and employers do not follow guidelines for the safe use of tools. When starting work in construction, the basic tools for the job will be mainly hand tools such as hammers, screwdrivers, chisels, scrapers, wrenches, trowels and spanners.

These tools should be cleaned, checked and maintained daily to make sure they are in good condition for work. Accidents and injuries may be prevented by:

* using the correct tool for the job – for example, you should never use a screwdriver or a file as a lever
* using the tool correctly – this includes using the right safety equipment, such as goggles
* checking tools for wear and tear – such as splinters on wooden handles
* maintaining tools correctly – for example sharpening chisels.

SAFE╋Y TIP

Stress and panic can cause accidents. If you are feeling stressed or anxious, stop what you are doing, take several deep breaths and, if possible, ask for help.

NA╎L IT

Find out more about avoiding slips and trips by visiting the Health and Safety Executive 'slips' and 'watch your step' websites:
www.hse.gov.uk/construction/slips/index.htm
www.hse.gov.uk/watchyourstep/index.htm

NA╎L IT

Find out more about using work equipment safely by viewing the Health and Safety Executive brochure on the following website:
http://www.hse.gov.uk/pubns/indg229.pdf
or you can obtain a free copy of *Use work equipment safely* – HSE publication from HSE Books.

Power tools may be operated by electricity or compressed air. These tools, and large plant and equipment such as scaffolds or forklift trucks, require specialised training.

Tools used in the construction industry

A wide range of tools and equipment is used in the construction industry including:

* **Hammers** – there are many different types of hammer: these tools may be used for driving in nails, applying force to a chisel or bending a piece of metal. Always check that the hammer head is firmly attached in hammers with a wooden handle. The handle should be splinter-free.

* **Saws** – used for cutting materials to shape. Again there are many types, such as hacksaws for cutting metal, and tenon saws for cutting and making timber joints.

* **Screwdrivers** – these have different sizes and shapes of tip. The main shapes are slotted – for general use – and cross-head.

* **Pliers** – these have serrated jaws for gripping and bending.

* **Ladders** – used to access working areas or platforms or for less than half an hour of work at a height. Make sure the ladder is in good condition with no cracks or spilled materials. Place it on firm, level ground at an angle of 75° and secure the ladder at the top and at the bottom before use.

* **Drills** – power tools with changeable end attachments (drill bits) used to make holes in materials.

TRY THIS

1. Find out and list the range of tools required for each of the following types of work:

   – brickwork

   – carpentry and joinery

   – painting and decorating

   – plumbing, heating, ventilation

   – electrical installation work

   – maintenance work

   – setting out procedures.

2. Select the occupation that you are most interested in and find out what safe-working checks and procedures apply to using these tools.

3. Practise using the tools selected, following all safe-working checks, methods and procedures, including cleaning and routine maintenance of the tools.

Work activities and environments

When you have learned the skills of your chosen career, the next step is to apply those skills in a variety of different contexts – that is, different environments and projects. Some of these environments have additional associated hazards that you may not have experienced in a workshop situation.

On-site hazards

A construction site is a busy place, and even on the most safely and efficiently run site there is potential for harm if staff are not both careful and alert. Accidents and injuries could result from, for example, vehicle collisions or falling materials. You need to be aware of all the other people working on-site and what they are doing, what equipment they are using, what impact their work could have on you and how your work could have an impact on them. You should know:

* which are the correct vehicle and pedestrian routes around the site

* where power lines and power tools are being used

* where there is a water supply

* whether there are people working overhead

* which areas are used for storing chemicals

* which areas are used for hoisting materials to higher levels

* which access routes should be used inside the building.

Untidy sites

Construction management and health and safety experts take a lot of time and effort to assess health, safety and welfare issues on a construction site. The procedures and work instructions for the site are written to ensure that all workers are safe. The level of risk associated with hazards on-site is greatly increased if the site is not maintained according to work instructions. Good housekeeping, including tidying away tools, equipment and materials and disposing of rubbish correctly, are as important as using the right PPE and operating tools and equipment correctly.

Manual handling

Manual handling includes pushing, pulling, lifting and lowering. Severe, and often permanent, back injury can result from handling loads incorrectly. You should never attempt to move a load weighing more than 20 kg by yourself. When lifting and moving a load, follow the steps for safe manual handling. These are as follows:

1. Make sure you have a clear path to your destination before you pick up the load.

2. Keep your back straight, bend your knees to pick up the load.

3. Use the leg and thigh muscles to straighten the body.

4. Keep your arms close to the body and avoid twisting.

5. Move steadily without rushing.

6. Keep your back straight and bend your knees to place the load down carefully.

DRILL DOWN

Make a list of 'good housekeeping' tasks that you should do at the end of each working day.

Working at heights

The Work at Height Regulations 2005 include the following **hierarchy of control** measures for dealing with the risks of working at heights:

* avoid working at height (Reg 6(2))

* prevent any person falling (Reg 6(3))

* use an existing place of work which complies with Schedule 1 (Reg 6(4) (a) (i))

* use work equipment (Reg 6(4) (b))

* mitigate (reduce) falls by using work equipment to minimise the distance and consequences of a fall (Reg 6(5) (a) (i))

* mitigate falls by using work equipment to minimise the consequences of a fall (Reg 6(5) (a) (ii))

* where the work equipment selected does none of the above, provide additional training and instruction or other suitable measures (Reg 6(5) (b)).

Equipment used for working at heights for any period of time longer than 30 minutes includes:

* a **scissor lift** – this is a small vehicle with a safe platform with guard rails and toe bars that can be raised to different heights. A safety harness attaching the worker to the lift must be worn

* a **scaffold** – a structure built using metal pipes and boards by a qualified scaffolder. Check that a scaffold is safe to use:

  – the scaffold tubes should be plumb and level

  – there should be toe boards, braces, guardrails and scaffold boards

  – the scaffold should be accessed from a secure ladder.

Scaffolding

◘ Confined spaces

A confined space is any enclosed space where there is a risk of death or serious injury from hazardous substances such as toxic gas or dust, or dangerous conditions such as a lack of oxygen. Confined spaces include:

* storage tanks

* enclosed drains

* sewers

* open-topped chambers

* air conditioning or heating ducts

* poorly ventilated rooms.

You need confined space training and a permit to work to carry out tasks in a confined space.

◘ Working near vehicles and plant

Special care should be taken when working on a site where vehicles and **plant** are being used. Vehicles may need to manoeuvre in and out of different areas to load waste or drop supplies. Reversing vehicles should emit warning noises – so listen out for these!

Areas in which plant is operating should be cordoned off with safety barriers and tapes. Signs should be in place to warn workers on-site to keep clear. You need to be alert and find out the correct walkways and access routes on the site.

Vehicles and plant on a construction site may include:

* excavators

* dump trucks

* cranes

* bulldozers

* rollers

* scissor lifts.

NAIL IT

Find out more about safe work in confined spaces by viewing the Health and Safety Executive brochure online at the following website:
www.hse.gov.uk/pubns/indg258.pdf

Plant – machinery used on a construction site, for instance dump trucks and cranes.

An example of the heavy plant you will encounter on a construction site.

Materials

You should always check the Material Safety Data Sheet (MSDS) for any solid, liquid or gaseous materials you need to use in your work. The MSDS is supplied by the manufacturer and lists:

* the properties of the substance

* the method of use, such as level of dilution of liquid

* safety precautions and PPE

* emergency procedures

* disposal method.

DRILL DOWN

How many material safety data sheets can you find in your workplace or training workshop?

General

Synonyms:	cement
Use:	constituent of concrete, mortar
Molecular formula:	Main constituents are calcium silicates, aluminates, ferro-aluminates and sulphates. May contain traces of gypsum and chromium compounds.

CAS No: 65997-15-1
EINECS No:

Physical data

Appearance: odourless fine white to grey powder
Melting point:
Boiling point:
Vapour density:
Vapour pressure:
Density (g cm^3):
Flash point:
Explosion limits:
Auto-ignition temperature:

Stability

Stable. Will solidify over a period of hours if moistened or wet. Absorbs moisture from the air (and solidifies) over prolonged periods unless kept in a dry atmosphere.

Toxicology

Dust acts as a skin and respiratory irritant. Dust and wet cement act as a serious eye irritant. Long-term or repeated exposure may lead to contact dermatitis. Typical OES 8hr TWA 10mg/m^3 inhalable dust.

Risk phrases

(The meaning of any risk phrases which appear in this section is given here.)
R36 R37 R38.

Transport information

Non-hazardous for air, sea and road freight.

Personal protection

Avoid contact with skin and eyes. Use in a well-ventilated area.

Figure 3.1 The Material Safety Data Sheet (MSDS) for cement.

Medium density fibreboard (MDF)

MDF is softwood, bonded with formaldehyde-based synthetic resin. When machining MDF, the atmosphere becomes filled with wood dust carrying formaldehyde, which can be carried into the lungs.

Both dust and formaldehyde can cause respiratory irritation, dry throat, **rhinitis** and eye irritation as well as occupational skin disease. You need to use the recommended respiratory and eye protection when working with MDF.

> **Rhinitis** – inflammation of the nasal passages causing a runny nose.

Paint, paint solvents and thinners

Paint and paint solvents give off fumes and may be flammable or harmful to the respiratory system. Painting activities should always be done in a well-ventilated and dust-free area. Paint and paint solvents and thinners may also cause irritation to the eyes or skin and should never be **ingested**.

* Turpentine (turps) is flammable and can cause respiratory problems if breathed in over long periods.

Mineral spirits is used as a thinner for many types of paint. It can cause conjunctivitis, eye damage, nausea, vomiting, diarrhoea, headache and dizziness and **dermatitis**.

> **Dermatitis** – a skin condition where the affected area (often the hands) becomes red, itchy and sore. The skin can sometimes crack and get infected.

Adhesives

Wood glue, such as epoxy resin, and other adhesives emit strong fumes that may cause dizziness and nausea. Some can also cause skin irritation and dermatitis. Tile adhesive, for example, contains a small amount of chromium, which is known to cause dermatitis. Some organisations have banned the use of adhesives (and cement) containing chromium.

DRILL DOWN

What is the correct way to wash your hands after working with potential contaminants?

Lead

Lead is a naturally occurring heavy metal used in some paints and solders. Lead will accumulate in the body of you breathe in lead dust or vapours or accidentally ingest lead (for example eating after working with lead solder without washing your hands).

If the level of lead in the body reaches a high level, you may suffer symptoms such as headaches, nausea and anaemia. If exposure to lead continues, the symptoms are more serious, for example kidney, nerve or brain damage. Special extractors and respirators should be used when working with significant levels of lead.

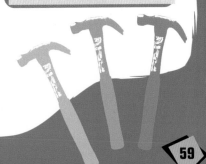

NAIL IT

Find out more about asbestos by reading the advice to employees on the HSE website: www.hse.gov.uk/asbestos/employees.htm

Asbestos

Asbestos is the greatest single cause of workplace deaths in the UK. It is a naturally occurring substance used in the past, before the lethal effects were known, to produce fireproof construction materials. These materials break down over time, forming asbestos dust which, if inhaled, can be lethal. Asbestos materials can still be found in many old buildings.

If you think a substance or material may contain asbestos, leave it alone and ask your supervisor for help. Working with and removal of asbestos may only be undertaken by specially trained people.

WHAT WOULD YOU DO?

What precautions would you take if your work involved using the following materials? Research the advice on the manufacturer's leaflet or Material Safety Data Sheet.

a) Concrete

b) Materials containing asbestos (removal)

c) Lead solder

d) Lead-based paint (removal)

e) MDF

f) Paint thinner

What hazardous materials do you come into contact with in the construction occupation you are most interested in? The materials could be dust or fumes arising from using or working on the materials – for example, wood dust. List at least three hazardous materials and make a work plan that must be followed when using these materials.

EVIDENCE

Research two accidents or incidents in the construction industry.

Ask your supervisor, teacher or trainer to arrange for you to visit two construction industry workplaces and interview the health and safety officer about past accidents or incidents. If this is not possible, use either the internet or accident or incident case studies from construction industry magazines, educational videos or other resources. Check with your supervisor, teacher or trainer that the case studies you have chosen are suitable.

For each accident or incident, compile a short report, including illustrations, such as a labelled sketch of the work area, covering:

* details of the activity involved and how the accident happened

* the precautions that are usually taken during the particular activity involved

* the cause of the accident

* the outcomes of the accident (injury or damage)

* how the accident may have been avoided

* any changes in procedures or tools, equipment or materials used, as a result of the accident.

Working safely in construction and building services crafts

In this section you will learn about...

* **safe work planning**

* **workplace precautions**

* **risk assessments.**

A safe worker is aware of risks and hazards and of the safety precautions and PPE required for different tasks in their job. A safe worker will also plan tasks carefully, checking all the correct procedures, work instructions and methods, materials, tools and equipment.

Planning for work

Safety hazards are reduced when work is planned carefully, taking into account all the known risks and following all the recommended safety procedures.

Tool-box talks

These are very short safety training sessions – usually about 30 minutes – focusing on the safety aspects of a particular task. Construction Skills produce a set of 70 tool-box talks with a laminated card for each topic. The topics include:

* ladders

* lifting equipment

* noise control

* abrasive wheels

* risk assessments and method statements.

DRILL DOWN

Ask your supervisor, teacher or trainer to show you work plans for simple tasks in your chosen sector of the construction industry. Choose a different task that you can do and write your own work plan for the task.

NAIL IT

Find out more about tool-box talks by visiting the CITB Construction Skills website:
www.citb-constructionskills.co.uk/publications/product.asp?p=2

TRy THIS

Imagine that you are a safety officer, and that you are going to give a short 'tool-box talk' on one aspect of health and safety relevant to your chosen sector of the construction industry. Choose one health and safety topic, such as using ladders or manual handling. Prepare notes for your talk and practise a demonstration of safe work methods for your topic.

◖ Hazard identification

Hazard identification involves finding out all the ways that a person could be harmed when performing a task. You need to look at everything in the work area and assess everything in terms of whether injury or damage could be caused, no matter how unlikely.

case study

Chris is a joiner, working on the first and second fix of large construction projects using the usual joinery hand tools and power tools, such as chisels, circular saws, hammers and planers. The first fix includes jobs such as fitting floorboards, studwork partitions, stairwells and loft traps and tank stands. The second fix includes hanging doors, fixing skirting boards and architraves and finishing the staircase. Chris recently read an article about a joiner who fell through an unprotected stairwell, fracturing his spine and puncturing his lung. He says: 'I have to work at heights, such as in the loft and on scaffolds, so I need to protect myself from falls. I always check the equipment to make sure I am secured to a stable anchor-point when working at heights – I don't want the same thing to happen to me. I also protect myself from cuts when using sharp tools and from electrocution when using power tools by following safe practices and wearing the appropriate PPE. I use good quality work boots, a hard hat, visor, goggles, mask, gloves and ear defenders.'

Questions and activities

1. Discuss with your colleagues, teacher, supervisor or trainer:

   a) Which parts of Chris's job do you think present the most risk?

   ✱ The first fix?

   ✱ The second fix?

   b) Which particular tasks are the most hazardous?

2. Discuss with your colleagues, teacher, supervisor or trainer the prevention methods Chris should use to avoid the following accidents:

   ✱ falls from height

   ✱ cuts from tools

   ✱ electrocution from power tools.

   Note down the results of your discussion.

3. Select five other construction occupations and research the PPE used in each. List each occupation, the PPE used and the reason why it is used.

Significant hazards in the construction industry include:

* ladders

* towers

* fragile roofs

* untidiness (the main cause of slips and trips)

* road traffic

* site transport

* lifting

* cement (causes dermatitis)

* noise

* power tools (cause hand-arm vibration syndrome).

Risk assessment compliance

A risk assessment will consider not only the immediate effect of hazards but also their effect over long periods of time. It is important to follow the recommended safety procedures at all times and wear the correct protective equipment.

Workplace precautions

Each workplace has a health and safety system to ensure that dangers are minimised. The system ranges from the manager's review of accidents that have occurred, and decisions to change procedures or introduce new ones, to the improvement of work methods or purchase of new types of protective equipment or tools to use on-site.

Control

Many risks are unavoidable but can be controlled. Workplace precautions to reduce hazards are based on the hierarchy of controls.

The Work at Height Regulations 2005 include the following hierarchy of control measures for dealing with the risks of working at heights:

* avoid working at height (Reg 6(2))

* prevent any person falling (Reg 6(3))

  – use an existing place of work which complies with Schedule 1 (Reg 6(4) (a) (i))

  – use work equipment (Reg 6(4) (b))

* mitigate (reduce) falls by using work equipment to minimise the distance and consequences of a fall (Reg 6(5) (a) (i))

* mitigate falls by using work equipment to minimise the consequences of a fall (Reg 6(5) (a) (ii))

* where the work equipment selected does none of the above, provide additional training and instruction or other suitable measures (Reg 6(5) (b)).

Other risk assessment compliance may involve:

* rotating tasks

* sticking to time limits on the use of particular equipment.

These strategies may be aimed at reducing exposure to dust, chemicals, noise or vibration, all of which have effects that accumulate over time.

Working with COSHH and PUWER risk assessments

The five steps to risk assessment are:

1. Identify the hazards – this involves working though all the ways in which machinery, equipment and materials are used, and, in the case of materials – especially chemicals – storage, decanting and dilution.

2. Work out who could be harmed and how the harm could occur – think of all possible scenarios.

3. Evaluate the risk and select the best precautions according to the hierarchy of controls.

4. Record the findings and implement preventative procedures.

5. Monitor the workplace for accidents and incidents and review the risk assessment and procedures on a regular basis.

A risk assessment for chemicals in the workplace should list all the possible chemicals and contaminants in a workplace, including dust, fumes and vapours.

Hazard controls

Hazard control for chemicals and contaminants may include:

* ventilation and extraction requirements

* respiratory protection

* length of exposure

* frequency of exposure

* monitoring the effectiveness of the controls.

TRY THIS

Ask your supervisor or trainer to help you arrange visits to three different work areas to assess the hazards.

For each work area, draw up a table and list the hazards, the risks associated with each hazard, and the precautions that are, or could be, taken to prevent accidents or injury. For example:

Work area: Site Office		
Hazard	**Risk**	**Precautions**
Trailing extension cable for laptop computer	Trips and falls	Tape the cable to the wall

EVIDENCE

What is meant by the hierarchy of controls ?

Using examples of real hazards in the workplace, prepare a short report to demonstrate your understanding of the hierarchy of controls and how this can be applied to remove or reduce hazards in the construction workplace.

COSHH and PUWER risk assessments

Collect copies of at least one COSHH and one PUWER risk assessment relevant to your workplace, workshop or sector of the construction industry.

Summarise one of each type of risk assessment in your own words.

Emergency procedures

In this section you will learn about...

* **what to do in an emergency**

* **accident reporting**

* **first aid.**

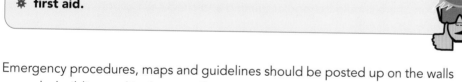

Emergency procedures, maps and guidelines should be posted up on the walls around a building and in the site office on-site. These procedures include:

* evacuation procedures and maps

* map showing the location of first aid equipment

* map showing the location of firefighting equipment

* guidelines on the use of firefighting equipment

* emergency services telephone numbers

* CPR (cardio-pulmonary resuscitation) reference guide.

SAFE✚Y TIP

Don't try to be the hero if you come across a fire. If you are in any doubt about being able to deal with it, GET OUT and seek help.

◙ Firefighting equipment

Fire is always a danger on building sites, as there are a lot of flammable materials around. If you have to deal with a fire, you must act swiftly and sensibly. If it is a large fire, evacuate the area and seek help. If it is a small fire, it might be possible to put it out quickly. Firefighting equipment that might be available to you includes:

* fire-resistant blankets
* buckets of sand or water
* fire extinguishers

Be sure to use the right fire extinguisher for the job. They are specifically designed to deal with particular types of fire. Check the instructions on the extinguisher before using.

Make sure you know which fire extinguisher to use for any particular type of fire.

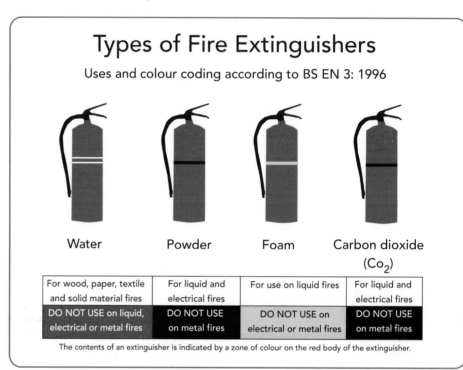

Types of Fire Extinguishers

Uses and colour coding according to BS EN 3: 1996

Water	Powder	Foam	Carbon dioxide (Co2)
For wood, paper, textile and solid material fires	For liquid and electrical fires	For use on liquid fires	For liquid and electrical fires
DO NOT USE on liquid, electrical or metal fires	DO NOT USE on metal fires	DO NOT USE on electrical or metal fires	DO NOT USE on metal fires

The contents of an extinguisher is indicated by a zone of colour on the red body of the extinguisher.

Emergencies

All construction sites should have emergency procedures, as listed above. In addition, there should be regular training and checks to cover:

* evacuation plans and practices
* alarm location
* alarm checks
* methods for contacting emergency services
* escape routes
* first aid.

TRy THIS

Find out the evacuation plan for your area of the workplace or your workshop or training room. Study the evacuation plan and learn the correct exit route. Arrange with your teacher, supervisor or trainer to conduct a group activity for practising evacuation procedures. This activity may also involve role-playing a scenario in which there is a fire.

Accident procedure

In most cases, as an entry-level employee in the industry, your role in the case of an accident will be:

* to apply basic first aid (if you feel confident to do so)
* alert the trained first aider or emergency services.

Duty to report incidents and dangerous conditions

Any potentially dangerous situation, even where an accident or injury is avoided, must be reported so that steps can be taken to avoid future problems.

Under the Reporting of Incidents, Diseases and Dangerous Occurrences Regulations (RIDDOR), 1995, all work-related accidents, diseases and dangerous occurrences must be reported by:

* phone – on 0845 3009923
* internet – complete the relevant form on the RIDDOR site
* hard-copy form – complete the relevant hard-copy form and send it by:
  - fax on 0845 3009924
  - post to Incident Contact Centre, Caerphilly Business Park, Caerphilly, CF83 3GG

The report will be dealt with by the area office of the Health and Safety Executive.

NAIL IT

For further information about the requirements of RIDDOR, visit the website www.riddor.gov.uk/info.html

Procedures in the event of fire or other emergencies

These procedures differ from site to site and should be included in induction training when starting work, and in site induction training when starting work at a new site.

First aid

First aid is the immediate simple assistance that can be given to the victim of an accident by a person who is not medically trained. It is intended to:

* keep the person alive until medical aid arrives
* prevent the injuries from getting worse
* help the person to recover from the injury.

NAIL IT

For more about basic first aid, look at this website. www.bbc.co.uk/health/first_aid_action/getting_started_pg2.shtml

First aid action plan

Follow the DRABC steps below to ensure that you keep yourself safe while checking the casualty for life signs and providing or seeking assistance:

* **Danger** – check for hazards and remove them where it is safe to do so.
* **Response** – is the casualty conscious?
* **Airway** – make sure the casualty's airway is clear.
* **Breathing** – is the casualty breathing?
  - if yes, place the casualty in the **recovery position**
  - if no, start, or find someone to apply, cardio-pulmonary resuscitation (CPR)

* **Circulation** – does the casualty have a pulse?
  - if yes, place casualty in the recovery position
  - if no, start, or find someone to apply CPR.

Contents of a basic first aid box

Different types of worksite will have different types and quantities of first aid items, depending on the nature of the work and the types of injury that occur most frequently. A basic first aid box should contain the following items:

* a first aid leaflet for basic advice
* at least 20 sterile adhesive dressings
* two sterile eye pads
* four sterile triangular bandages
* six safety pins
* six medium and two large sterile, unmedicated wound dressings
* one pair of disposable gloves.

First aid boxes should not contain any medication.

Typical contents of a workplace first aid box

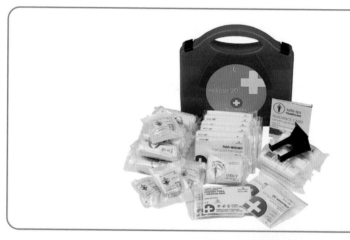

WHAT WOULD YOU DO?

If an accident occurred in your workplace or workshop would you know what to do?

Find out the correct immediate first aid procedures that you should follow in each of the following scenarios:

* A person using a power tool suffers an electric shock and collapses to the floor.

* Someone has an asthma attack.

* A person slips on some spilt liquid and lands on a concrete floor near some steps, receiving a severe bump to the head from the corner of a step.

* Someone using a sharp tool applies too much pressure, causing the tool to slip and penetrate quite deeply into the left hand.

EVIDENCE

Research current incident and accident statistics on the HSE website:

* www.hse.gov.uk/statistics/nationalstats.htm

* www.hse.gov.uk/statistics/industry/construction.htm

Compare the overall statistics to those for the construction industry.

Write a short report on accidents and incidents in the construction industry.

Complete an incident reporting form.

Download an incident reporting form F2508 from the HSE website:
http://rweb1.nbapp.com/hse/riddor.nsf/F2508?OpenFrameSet

Complete the form for an imaginary accident or incident, for example one of those listed in the previous activity.

Personal effectiveness

At the end of this unit you should be able to...

* present a personal audit of your job-related skills

* list a range of jobs that suit your skills, attributes and interests

* identify your strengths in relation to your career choices and plan strategies to build on these as part of your career action plan

* identify weaknesses needing improvement in relation to your career choices and plan strategies to make progress in these areas as part of your career action plan

* prepare a factual and positive personal statement, letter and CV for job applications.

4

Unit overview

How effective are you at describing and explaining your own strengths, skills and experience? The first question many employers ask at a job interview is 'Could you tell me a little bit about yourself?' In this situation, what would you say? Talking and writing about your skills, abilities and attributes in a factual and positive way is one of the keys to getting a job and pursuing a great career. In order to do this, you need to explore and evaluate various aspects of yourself including:

* education and training

* personality type

* physical skills

* communication skills

* interpersonal skills and behaviour

* interests

* goals

* ambitions.

When you have a good understanding of these aspects, you can develop effective ways of expressing yourself and conveying this information to prospective employers.

Getting on well with your colleagues is a vital skill at work.

Personal audit

In this section you will learn about...

* **how to assess your own skills and weaknesses**

* **how to create a good impression**

* **how to get on with work colleagues**

* **how to behave appropriately at work.**

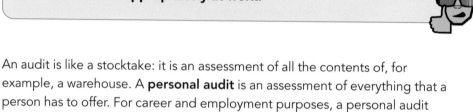

An audit is like a stocktake: it is an assessment of all the contents of, for example, a warehouse. A **personal audit** is an assessment of everything that a person has to offer. For career and employment purposes, a personal audit means an assessment of everything about yourself that may be relevant to the career you choose and the jobs you decide to apply for.

Vocational skills

Vocational skills are those that are particularly relevant to performing the tasks in a work occupation. Some skills learned in one type of occupation are transferable, and can be equally relevant in other occupations. For example, serving customers in a shop is a vocational skill related to the retail sector. However, the ability to interact well with customers is a useful skill in all occupations where you may have direct contact with the client. Imagine you are involved as a building and construction worker in a home renovation and are in constant contact with the homeowner. Your skills in dealing with customers could be very useful.

Work-related experiences

Begin your personal audit by assessing all your past work-related experiences and the tasks that you performed in these. Then assess the types and level of skill that you achieved as a result of each experience. For example, you may have had:

* part-time jobs, such as a newspaper round or working in a shop

* work experience arranged by your school

* voluntary work for a local community group, charity or even a neighbour.

Skills you acquire at school are also transferable to the workplace. These include numerical skills, report writing and the ability to follow instructions. School sports encourage teamworking and spatial understanding.

Practical qualifications

Any qualifications that you have, even those that are not related to the building and construction industry, show a prospective employer that you are a determined person who will stick at something until you achieve a goal.

Aside from school or college exams, qualifications that you may have achieved include:

* first aid certificate

* sports certificates

* sign language certificate

* music or dancing certificates

* Duke of Edinburgh award

* scouting, guiding, Sea Cadet or CCF awards.

Physical skills

Physical skills range from gross motor skills, using the larger muscles in the body, to fine motor skills, using the smaller muscles, particularly in the hands and fingers.

Gross motor skills involve the strength and fitness required for lifting and placing bricks, stones and timbers.

Fine motor skills involve the precision and manual dexterity that may be required for matching patterns of tiles or wallpaper.

Physical skills and experience relevant to the building and construction industry include:

* working with your hands – this means manual dexterity and crafting abilities such as painting, trowel work and working with wood

* spatial understanding – this means understanding the relationship between different objects or events in terms of distance, order, size, time and volume, such as:

  - interpreting schedules and timetables

  - reading plans and maps

  - having a good sense of 3D space

  - working out how things fit together

  - drawing and drawing interpretation abilities – this means making sketches and understanding scale drawings, plans and maps

  - good hand-eye coordination – this means that your hands follow where your eye wants them to go. People with good hand-eye coordination are not clumsy. Jugglers have good hand-eye coordination.

  - fitness and the ability to climb ladders and work at heights – some people have vertigo, or a fear of heights

  - good eyesight – there are limitations of entry into some building and construction jobs if you are partially sighted or colour-blind.

TRY THIS

Make an assessment of your physical skills by attempting activities in the following categories:

* gross motor skills, for example:

  – playing football or netball

  – climbing up and down a ladder (make sure you do this safely)

  – jog round the school playing field or local park and see how long it is before you get tired.

* fine motor skills, for example:

  – doing jigsaw puzzles or making small models

  – painting edge lines neatly

  – threading a needle.

* drawing and sketching, for example:

  – make a plan of the training room or workshop

  – make a three-dimensional sketch of a small building

  – draw a piece of furniture, such as a chair or table.

If you are not sure how to assess yourself, ask someone else, such as a another student or your supervisor, teacher or trainer, to judge your competence.

Personal skills

Most of us make assumptions about people within the first few seconds of meeting them, based on the way they look. For example, if you owned a business and a person turned up for a job interview dressed scruffily and with a slouching **posture** – you would probably assume that they weren't that keen on getting the job. The way you present yourself to a person for the first time forms a lasting impression, which could be hard to change.

TH!NK ABOUT

Types of dressing style include: formal, uniform, smart, smart-casual, casual – and scruffy! What would you wear for each of these styles? Think of an occasion for each type of dressing style.

Appearance

In general, your appearance should be clean, neat, simple and in keeping with the general style of people doing a similar type of work. Make sure it is appropriate for the occasion. Your appearance should be more formal for an interview, or in work clothes to do a particular job.

Dress code

Each company will have a policy on the type of clothing to be worn at work; this is called the dress code. For site work, the main consideration is safety, and the clothing worn on-site should be durable and protective. In offices, one of the considerations is making a good impression on the clients.

Posture

The bones of your body hold you up and joints link bones together. In correct alignment, the bones and joints function well. Your posture also gives an impression of your personality and attitude to life – a good posture suggests a confident and fit person, a poor posture gives the impression of someone who is not confident, not enthusiastic and not very fit. A poor posture can also affect your health and well-being.

Body language

Body language is communication using body movements, gestures and facial expressions, for example:

* tilting the head slightly to one side shows that you are interested

* shrugging your shoulders shows that you don't know or don't care.

You can tell a lot from someone's body language, which is often unconscious and reveals someone's inner feelings more than anything they might actually say. For instance, if the person you are talking to won't make eye contact, or is constantly looking around when you are speaking, it tells you that they are not really concentrating on you, no matter what they may actually be saying.

Crossing the arms across the chest is a defensive posture, but leaning towards you is an indication that the person is interested in you and what you are saying.

Try to make sure you use positive body language in interviews and with colleagues. Look people in the eye when you are having a conversation with them; try to appear neutral, rather than aggressive or defensive, in your stance and posture.

Avoid using wild or stabbing gestures.

> **Posture** – the alignment of your body, the way you hold yourself when you stand, sit and walk. The basis of a good posture is the 'neutral spine', when the body is relaxed and the ears, shoulders, hips, knees and ankles are in one straight line.

TRY THIS

With a partner, try using body language only to send the following messages:

* 'Come and look at this.'

* 'I am really confused.'

* 'Do you need any help?'

Can you communicate any other simple messages just with gestures?

How would you give the impression of being interested in what the other person is saying?

How do you give the impression that you are not at all interested in the other person's conversation?

Interpersonal skills

The way you interact with other people in the workplace depends on whether you know them well, or not at all, and whether or not they are senior to you in some way.

Your interactions with other people at work should always be polite, calm and pleasant. You may be more informal with people of your own age group, but people in the workplace with more experience and responsibility than you will expect a more formal and respectful approach.

◙ Getting on with people

Getting on with people involves good communication, using everyday politeness and good manners.

The reason for politeness and good manners is to enable you to communicate effectively with people you may not know or even like. It provides an effective way of exchanging information. This everyday politeness also involves a certain level of detachment – which means that you limit your conversation to what is necessary and keep personal information and opinions to the minimum.

◙ Relating to others in a work situation

Relating to and communicating with colleagues and customers at work includes:

* greeting and saying goodbye to clients and colleagues

* building team relations through friendly conversations

* giving and receiving information and/or instructions

* being open and receptive to others who might want to ask you questions

* discussing and resolving work-based problems

* asking for information or help.

All of these exchanges should be friendly and polite. There will always be some people at work that you like more than others, and you may choose to spend lunch breaks with friends that you make at work.

However, during working hours you must treat everyone with the same level of respect. This means:

* greeting everyone you meet – not ignoring anyone

* paying the same amount of attention and listening carefully to each work colleague

* including everyone close by in friendly workplace conversations – not excluding anyone.

TH!NK ABOUT

Examples of everyday polite conversation include:

– 'Good morning, how are you today?' – 'Fine thanks, and you?'

– 'Goodnight then, see you tomorrow.' – 'Yeah, good night. Have a good evening.'

How do you think you would politely greet a person who was interviewing you?

case study

Jen is trying to decide which career in the construction industry is best suited to her skills. She wants a career in one of the craft areas. She has excellent eyesight, works hard and loves working outdoors, but is a bit shy. She gets along fine with others, but prefers just to concentrate on her work. Jen is quite ambitious and wants to be a success. Being the only female in her family to try a career in this area, she wants to prove that she can do it. Jen has interviewed some construction industry workers and received the following advice:

'To work well as a bricklayer, a person should be friendly, trustworthy, enthusiastic and hardworking. The job is not suited to people who only see it as a way to make a living.'

'A site joiner needs to be down-to-earth and capable of communicating with everyone on the site. People who are work-shy or who cannot cope with extreme weather would not be suited to the job.'

'An installation electrician should be thoughtful and knowledgeable. It's not a job for people who are colour-blind.'

'A maintenance joiner needs to be proactive, outgoing and a good communicator. People who are a bit shy and cannot keep up a conversation would not enjoy the job.'

Questions and activities

1. Consider what you know about Jen, and then discuss with your colleagues, trainer, teacher or supervisor the advice given about the different careers. Note down how well you think Jen would be suited to each career, giving your reasons.

2. Think of five positive adjectives you would use to describe your own personality and attributes.

3. Think of the weather conditions you could expect on a building site. What would you describe as extreme weather conditions? Are you prepared to work in these conditions?

4. Think of all the people that a maintenance joiner may have to converse with when working on repairs in a block of flats. Could you keep up a conversation with every type of person that the maintenance joiner might come into contact with?

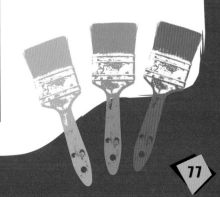

Behaviour

Your behaviour at work should show that you are a respectful, reliable, responsible and competent person. Safety is a vital concern in all building and construction industry organisations, and your behaviour at work should show your understanding of safety issues and knowledge of safety procedures.

Think about

How do you expect to be treated by your work colleagues? Think about the ways in which you think your work colleagues should show you respect. Do you respect your work colleagues in the same way?

Expected behaviour

In every workplace, employees are expected to interact positively and constructively with colleagues, supervisors and managers, clients and the general public and to work efficiently, effectively and safely. This expected behaviour includes:

* being on time and fit for work
* treating everyone with equal respect
* following procedures
* being alert and careful
* helping others when you have finished your tasks
* taking the opportunity to learn new skills.

Unacceptable behaviour

Unacceptable behaviour will usually result in a reprimand or formal disciplinary procedures. Most organisations operate a three warnings policy, where after each warning the employee is given help with, or strategies to modify, the behaviour. Unacceptable behaviour includes:

* unsafe working – this includes any actions that could result in an accident or injury, such as:
  – lack of care and attention
  – failure to follow correct procedures
  – 'clowning around' or 'mucking about' on site.

* bullying – this includes any unfair or unsuitable behaviour, such as:
  – excluding a person on purpose
  – petty criticism
  – interfering with work equipment or personal belongings
  – using abusive language or shouting
  – deliberately not telling a person important information
  – any unnecessary physical contact.

* sexual harassment – this includes unwanted sexual attention directed at a person based on their gender (male or female), such as:
  – inappropriate sexual comments and suggestions
  – unnecessarily touching or brushing against a person's body
  – staring and using sexually suggestive body language.

* discrimination – this includes any behaviour that results in people being treated differently due to their race, gender, sexual preference, ability or disability, such as:
  – always asking the female members of a team to make the tea

– never offering to team up with a person from a particular ethnic background.

You need to be aware of all these forms of unacceptable behaviour, but don't take any to the extreme – for example, if you have formed a friendship with someone at work, it is OK to pat them gently on the upper back or the arm, at appropriate times, without causing offence.

WHAT WOULD YOU DO?

What would you do in the following circumstances?

* Two of your work colleagues are 'clowning around' on site and you feel that this could get out of hand and result in an incident.

* One of your work colleagues keeps criticising your work and using abusive language.

Discuss your thoughts with your supervisor, teacher or trainer.

Modifying behaviour

As part of your own personal growth and development it is good to conduct a behaviour check every now and then. You should also reflect on your health and safety knowledge – think about any accidents, injuries or near misses that have occurred at work or college, or that you have read about in the papers or seen on the news, and consider how these could have been avoided.

TH!NK ABOUT

Think about your colleagues at work or college and assess how well you get on with each one. If you get on with one person less well than you do with the rest, try to analyse this and find out whether you could improve your tolerance, patience or attitude.

Interests

The way you choose to spend your spare time tells an employer a lot about your personality, your goals and your skills. When you are just starting out in the workforce, you do not have a lot of work experience to talk about when explaining what your skills and ambitions are. Your hobbies and interests may show that you use your time wisely, with a good balance between restful and active pastimes, and that you have talent in, and enthusiasm for, a variety of activities. Some of the skills you need in your hobbies may be transferable to the workplace.

Outdoor interests

Demonstrating that you have outdoor interests is important if you are aiming at a career that involves outdoor work. For example, if you play for a hockey or football team and practise and play in all weathers, an employer will be reassured about your ability to withstand a bit of weather on site. Outdoor activities may include:

* building a tree house

* gardening

* walking

* horse riding

* outdoor sports.

Indoor interests

People who enjoy working outdoors often choose a career in the building and construction industry – but not all the careers available in this industry involve outdoor work. If your preferred career involves mainly indoor work, then it is good to show an employer that you enjoy being indoors. These may include:

* interior decorating

* drawing

* making models

* reading.

Relating interests to work skills and attributes

Other interests and hobbies may include aspects that demonstrate a particular skill or ability to an employer, for example:

* an interest in travelling – shows an employer that you may be willing to work away from home

* an interest in drama, dance or musical performance – shows an employer that you are not shy and may be able to approach new clients or make presentations to clients.

EVIDENCE

Work skills

Make a list of all your past work experience, including voluntary work, casual jobs and work experience placements. List the skills you have developed and then consider each skill – is the skill transferable into your construction career? How?

Qualifications

Make a list of all your accomplishments, qualifications and certificates. For each qualification, list the work-related skills that this proves you have.

For example:

* Grade five piano:

  – Fine motor skills, hand-eye coordination, perseverance, commitment

* Clean driving licence (passed first time):

  – Good coordination, observation skills, commitment to study, perseverence.

Hobbies and interests

Make a list of all your spare-time activities, then:

* analyse the skills and abilities you use in each activity

* relate the skills and abilities to your chosen career.

Potential

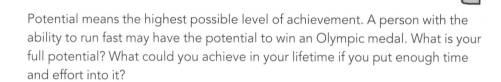

In this section you will learn about...

* **assessment of skills and potential**

* **matching skills and jobs**

* **forward planning.**

Potential means the highest possible level of achievement. A person with the ability to run fast may have the potential to win an Olympic medal. What is your full potential? What could you achieve in your lifetime if you put enough time and effort into it?

What do you hope to achieve during your working career?

Assessment

Psychometric tests are designed to measure skills, abilities, knowledge, aptitude and personality traits. Many employers use recruitment agencies and psychologists to assess short-listed job applicants for their suitability to do a particular job. Psychometric tests include tests for:

* numerical aptitude

* verbal aptitude

* spatial aptitude

* diagrammatical aptitude

* personal qualities and characteristics.

NAIL IT

Find out more about psychometric tests by visiting the 'A job today' website:
www.ajobtoday.co.uk/career home.aspx

TRY THIS

There are many psychometric tests available online for you to try out. Find two or three and use the results of these and your own self-assessment to identify:

- your strengths in relation to your career choices
- personal aspects needing improvement in relation to your career choices.

Keep a record of the results of the tests and use these results to identify areas where you can improve.

Try the same tests again in a few months' time and compare your results to see what progress you have made.

DRILL DOWN

Consider the skills and attributes required for jobs in your chosen career. You can research these by looking for job descriptions and adverts on the internet or in newspapers, or by asking for job descriptions for entry-level positions from well-known companies.

Self-assessment

A self-assessment involves listing the skills and attributes that are needed in a particular job, and then making a very honest assessment of your own ability in each of these areas. It is important to consider your own abilities in comparison with others of similar age, experience and ambitions.

Here is an example of the skills and interests listed in a job advertisement for a trainee painter and decorator:

To be a painter and decorator you should:

- be careful and methodical
- maintain a high standard of work
- be very practical
- have creative ability
- have good colour vision for mixing and matching paints
- be accurate
- have an eye for detail
- be able to work alone
- be able to work as part of a team
- be confident and safe working at heights
- be aware of health and safety issues.

Assessment by others

You might find some aspects of your personal skills and abilities hard to assess. In this case you can ask someone else, for example a teacher, work colleague, friend or relative to give you some honest feedback. Ask them how your abilities compare to the abilities of other people of similar age, experience, goals and ambitions. You could also look over any recent school or college results or reports, and any performance reviews you have participated in at work.

EVIDENCE

Assessment by others

Make a list of people who have some knowledge of your work-related skills, such as supervisors, experienced colleagues, teachers, trainers, family members and members of your community. Ask the people on your list whether they would be willing to help you in your career planning and personal development by filling in a questionnaire about your work-related skills. If the person would rather not do the questionnaire, just say thanks anyway, and try someone else. Some people may be too busy or may not feel confident in assessing your skills.

Your questionnaire should assess your ability in each work-related skill area and give a score out of 10, where 10 is excellent and 1 is not very good at all.

The questionnaire may include work-related skills such as:

* ability to listen and ask appropriate questions
* confidence levels
* ability to follow instructions
* good timekeeping
* administrative abilities
* customer focus
* getting on with other people (customers and colleagues)
* using initiative
* learning new skills.

Ask for suggestions for ways that you could improve if the score for a skill is less than 6.

Remember to thank everyone who completes a questionnaire for you.

DRILL DOWN

At an interview you could ask the employer what opportunities there would be to develop your strengths, for example: 'I am very creative and have achieved good results in art and design courses – what opportunities would there be for me to build on these skills in this company?'

Identify strengths to build on

When you review the results of your aptitude tests, self-assessment and assessment by others, look for the areas where you are strongest and show the most ability or aptitude. These are your strengths, and you can talk about these openly when asked at a job interview 'What are your strengths?' For example: 'I always did well at Maths at school, and achieved good results in my exams. I have also tried an on-line numerical aptitude test and achieved a high score in this.'

You could also ask questions of the employer based on your strengths, as it is always good to build your career around those skills and attributes that you are good at and that you enjoy.

Some skills and attributes that are important to employers include:

* ability to listen and ask appropriate questions
* appropriate level of confidence
* ability to follow instructions
* good timekeeping
* administrative abilities
* customer focus
* getting on with other people (customers and colleagues)
* using initiative
* learning new skills.

Identify personal weaknesses for improvement

Everyone has strengths and weaknesses, but some people never do anything about their weaker points. Personal aspects needing improvement could include:

* not listening attentively
* failing to ask questions when explanations are misunderstood
* difficulty in following instructions
* poor timekeeping
* dressing inappropriately
* not working as part of a team
* having difficulty working unsupervised or alone.

Your review of tests, self-assessment and assessment by others will also show where improvements could be made. You may need to focus your efforts, or undertake some training to address any weaknesses you identify. An employer will usually be impressed by a person who shows enough initiative to:

* identify aspects for improvement
* take steps to do something about it.

Matching strengths to job roles

It is important to choose the type of job and career that focuses on, and makes best use of, your strengths. Some jobs are very varied and may require a wide range of skills. Make sure you are aware of these, as well as the main skills needed for the job. For example:

* to be a building control officer, you should have excellent communication skills and be able to explain technical terms to members of the public

* a civil engineer needs to visualise and explain theoretical designs

* a stonemason needs to be creative to make decorative designs in or with the stone

* a carpenter needs good planning skills.

You could try ranking your strengths from your leading strength downwards, so that you look for a job that matches your major skills. You can also offer supplementary skills that could be useful in other aspects of the job. For instance if you are a skilled painter but are also quite good at maths, you might look at starting your own business and doing your own quotes and accounts.

TRY THIS

To assess your strengths and weaknesses, think about the skills you need at work, and for each one make a self-assesssment of:

* how much you enjoy practising a particular skill

* how good you are at a particular skill.

Rate these on a scale of one to five where:

5 = I really enjoy doing this / I am really good at doing this

4 = I quite enjoy doing this / I am quite good at doing this

3 = I don't mind doing this / I am neither good nor bad at doing this

2 = I don't like doing this / I am not very good at doing this

1 = I really don't like doing this / I am not at all good at doing this

Make a table for your assessment and add up the score for each skill

Example table:

Skill	Enjoyment	How good at it?	Total
Drawing	4	3	7
Estimating	2	4	6
Talking to customers	5	3	8

Discuss the results of your self-assessment with your colleagues, supervisor or trainer.

EVIDENCE

Matching your strengths to particular jobs

Using the information you have gathered so far about your work skills and preferences, find at least two job descriptions from newspapers or the internet which would suit your skills.

Action plan

An action plan sets down the steps you have decided to take to start and progress in your chosen career. If you want to achieve your full potential, you need a plan. You need to commit yourself to the plan – that is, to decide that you really are going to do it. Then you need to take action. Nothing will happen if you don't!

My career action plan for the next six months		
Goal 1: Improve my knowledge of the theory in my course and my performance in tests		
Action	**Timeframe**	**Outcome**
Find a mentor or coach to help me	by July	
Commit one extra hour per week to study	for four months	
Goal 2: Improve a particular practical skill that I find difficult		
Action	**Timeframe**	**Outcome**
Ask trainer to suggest tasks I can practise at home	by August	
Commit two hours on the weekend to practice	3 weeks	
Goal 3: Complete a few personality and aptitude tests on the internet		
Action	**Timeframe**	**Outcome**
Ask trainer to recommend websites	by October	
Commit one hour on the weekend to do the tests	2 weeks	
Goal 4: Find out what skills and abilities employers are asking for in my area of interest		
Action	**Timeframe**	**Outcome**
Ring up for job descriptions for advertised vacancies	by end Nov.	
Check internet job sites	by end Nov.	

Figure 4.1 Example of an action plan.

Long-term and short-term goals

A goal is something you want to achieve. Your ultimate goal might be to run a company with ten staff – but this is several years down the line. You need to break that down into smaller and smaller goals until you have a set of goals for the next few weeks.

For example:

* if you want to find a job in carpentry, one goal would be to make a list of ten carpentry companies in the local area that have a good reputation

✳ if you want to improve your painting skills, see if you can do a painting job at home or for a friend. Take a photograph of the finished work to use as evidence of your work. You can build pieces of evidence like this into a **portfolio** which you can show to prospective employers. We will talk more about your portfolio later.

Medium- to long-term goals might include successfully completing your BTEC course and getting a particular grade, getting your first job in construction and reaching a particular salary level.

Think about the benefits of each goal and write these down to remind you:

✳ why you are working on each goal

✳ what you could miss out on if you lose commitment.

◩ Action plan content

In terms of your career your action plan may include:

✳ short-term goals:

  – workplace skills improvement

  – workplace knowledge improvement

  – building networks and contacts

  – gathering information about your career, such as new methods and technology, and current projects locally, nationally and worldwide.

✳ timeframe for achievement of each goal:

  – over the next four weeks I am going to practise and improve my estimating skills

  – by the end of next month I will improve the accuracy and quality of my sketches

  – in the next six weeks, I will review all the industry magazines related to my work and take out a subscription to the one I like best

  – in the next three months I will attend a workshop or seminar related to my work.

Make sure that you have some method for reminding yourself of the steps you need to take each day, each week or each month in order to reach your goals.

EVIDENCE

Action plan
Using the information in this section and the work from the activities you have completed, create an action plan for the next six months.

◖ Evaluation

Check your action plan at the end of every week and assess your progress on each goal. If you have not accomplished what you set out to do, think about your commitment to this goal:

* What was the objective of the goal?

* Do you still want to achieve this objective?

* Is there another way to achieve the same objective?

EVIDENCE

Put the actions you need to take for each goal during the coming week into a diary or list so that you have a scheduled time to work on each goal. This will not only act as a reminder of what you intend to do, but also as a record of your achievements. You will gain a great sense of satisfaction from being able to tick off each goal as you achieve it.

Personal statement and portfolio

In this section you will learn about...

* collecting and preparing evidence for employers

* preparing a CV

* applying for jobs

* preparing for an interview.

A **personal statement** is a summary, with evidence, of all the work skills, knowledge and experience that you could offer to an employer. It is a good idea to keep a folder to record work-related accomplishments and to keep copies of all relevant paperwork (keep the original copy separately). Then you can pick and choose which ones to mention, or include a copy of, in an application for a job.

A **portfolio** is a record of all the activities undertaken to prepare for and apply for work. This could include lists of companies called in relation to job vacancies, preparation for interviews and letters of application for particular jobs.

Personal statement

Your personal statement includes material you have prepared or gathered to present to employers to show what skills, experience and attributes you have, and also your career goals and ambitions.

Curriculum vitae (CV)

A **curriculum vitae** (sometimes called a **résumé**) is a list of all your educational, training and employment history and achievements. Your CV should also include your personal and contact details. A CV is a way of putting as much information about yourself as possible on paper so that it is easy to scan and pick out details. It is the next best thing to interviewing you.

A CV is divided into six sections:

* Personal information, including:
    – full name
    – residential address
    – correspondence address (if different)
    – telephone numbers: business hours and after-hours
    – email address
    – date and place of birth
    – nationality.

* Career objective – this is a chance to make an impression with your commitment and determination.

* Education and training:
    – names of schools or institutions (start with the most recent)
    – level of schooling reached
    – certificates, licences and dates obtained
    – specialised knowledge/workplace training.

* Work experience: list each job including voluntary work and work experience. Start with the most recent and give the following information:
    – the date you started and the date you left
    – title of your position
    – name of employer or organisation
    – duties and responsibilities of your position
    – achievements.

* Other activities – include any work skills that you use in pursuing these activities, for example organising trips, leading a team:
    – membership of community or sporting organisations
    – interests and hobbies.

* References – give the names of two people who know you well, ideally one personal reference and one work/college reference.

Résumé – (pronounced: rez- you-may) this is a summary of your personal and contact details and a list of all your educational, training and employment history and achievements. In the UK, this is more usually called a CV.

TH!NK ABOUT

To create your CV you need to think about how to sum up your career and other experiences that may be relevant to your future.

TH!NK ABOUT

If you don't have British or EU nationality then you must provide evidence that you have permission to work in the UK, for instance a work permit or visa.

Christine Jameson
20 Cheadle Road
Manchester M22 4JJ
Tel: (0161) 369 2468
Email: ChrisJ@hotmail.com

DOB: 16/06/85

PROFILE:
A junior carpenter with a range of experience in the construction industry. Able to work on own initiative and as part of a team. First-class analytical, design and problem-solving skills. Dedicated to maintaining high quality standards.

CAREER HISTORY:
2006 – to date
WILMOT DIXON LIMITED: on-site carpenter

2004 – 2006
ANGLIAN WINDOWS LIMITED: trainee carpenter

TRAINING:
Various courses including: Quality Assurance, The BS5750 Quality Approach.

QUALIFICATIONS:
BTEC Construction - distinction.

6 GCSEs.

ADDITIONAL INFORMATION:
Driving Licence: Full, clean.

INTERESTS:
Hockey, Grand Prix racing, physical fitness – gym.

Figure 4.2 Example of a CV.

TH!NK ABOUT

Who will you put on your CV as a referee? Look back at the activity on 'assessment by others', and the questionnaires completed.

⮞ References

Wherever you work, whether it is work experience, voluntary work, casual or temporary work, it is a good idea to ask the supervisor or manager if you can list them as a referee on your CV or résumé. When you apply for a new job, the employer will ring your referees and ask them about your skills and your attitude to work. You cannot put a person's name and contact details on your CV without asking them first.

Portfolio

You need to gather a portfolio of material to provide evidence of your preparation for applying for jobs suited to your skills and attributes.

Telephone skills

You need to prepare telephone scripts for calling employers:

* about an advertised vacancy
* about the possibility of future vacancies.

Before making a phone call to an employer about an advertised job:

* research the details of the job – do you have the required skills and abilities?
* find out about the size and operations of the company
* make sure you talk to the right person – if you don't know the name of the person ask for:
  - the personnel manager, or
  - the person in charge of hiring people doing the job you are interested in
* make sure you have a pen and paper
* note down all the questions you want to ask.

Application forms

Some employers have standard application forms to be filled in. It is a good idea to practise filling these in correctly. If you do have to fill in a form, make a photocopy and fill that in first. If you don't have access to a photocopier, fill in the form in pencil first, and only ink it in when you are happy with all your answers. It is a good idea to photocopy your completed application, if you can, so that you can refer to it if you are called for interview.

TRY THIS

Calling employers

Find at least three companies or organisations you would like to work for. Write a short telephone script for making calls to these organisations asking whether you can send in your CV for future jobs. Call the employers and note down the details of the person you should send your CV to, and the address.

Application forms

Ask your supervisor or trainer to help you to collect at least two samples of job application forms from local employers in the construction industry. Practise filling in these application forms.

Letter of application

You should always write a covering letter to accompany a CV or application form. An application letter should include the following information:

- the title and reference number of the job you are applying for
- the place where the job was advertised
- the reason for your interest in the job
- a summary of evidence that you have the skills for the job
- the reasons why you want a job with this company in particular
- your willingness to attend an interview
- your contact details.

Some employers specifically ask for a handwritten letter or application form. Be sure to do this if requested. If you don't the employer will probably bin your application without even looking at it. They do this to check how legible (readable) and tidy your handwriting is, so make sure you do not scrawl.

If they do not state they want a handwritten application, then it makes a good impression, if possible, to type or word-process your letter. If you are using a computer, then it's a good idea to spell-check your work. No matter what, always proofread (critically read through) your letter to check for any mistakes, or even better, get someone else to check it for you. If you find any errors, it's in your best interest to correct them, even if this means writing out the letter again.

Preparation for interviews

You need to create the best possible first impression at an interview. You can do this by being well-prepared and well-presented.

You need to consider all of the following:

- **grooming** – this should be clean, neat, simple and conventional
- **attitude** – present your good attitude through confident, but not over-confident body language (eye-contact, firm handshake, good posture) and by being positive (smile, nod, show interest)
- **punctuality** – be early. Practise getting to the location, allow time for traffic problems on the actual day, find somewhere locally to have a tea or coffee, relax (and go to the loo!) near the location of the interview before you go into the building
- **paperwork** – make sure you have copies of your CV, letter, application form, certificates, references and any other relevant documents.

In preparation for a job interview you should be ready to answer the following types of question:

- What are the trends in the industry?
- What is your opinion of these trends?
- What do you know about the company?
- What is the scope of the company's operations?
- How well is it doing?
- Is it highly regarded?

* What do you think of it?

* What do you know about the particular department or section that the job is in?

* What is its role?

* Why do you want to work in it?

* What is involved in the actual job?

* Can you do it?

* Why would you enjoy it?

* Are you right for the job?

* What can you offer that others might not?

EVIDENCE

Create your CV

Using the advice in this section and on the career websites listed below, create your own CV.

* Careers portal website: www.careersportal.co.uk

* Go job site website: www.gojobsite.co.uk/career/

Using the job descriptions that you found in the activities in the previous section, or two new job descriptions, write two letters of application to the employer. You may choose to post these off with your CV.

TRY THIS

Practice interviews

Ask your supervisor or trainer to help you to role-play practice interviews for the two jobs you have applied for. Make sure that you take the time to prepare for the role-play interviews according to the advice earlier in this section.

Social responsibility at work

At the end of this unit you should be able to...

* investigate environmental issues in workplaces

* explain the environmental factors that are important to a chosen job role

* explain steps that may be taken to minimise environmental impacts

* explore how the law affects people in work

* describe the laws that apply to particular jobs

* explain why some work-related laws may be more important than others.

5

Unit overview

In this unit, you will find out how you can be socially responsible at work. Through the activities and assignments in the unit you will explore ways in which you could apply socially responsible actions to a particular job role.

Social responsibility means being aware of the impact of your actions, or lack of action, on the health and well-being of yourself, other people and on the environment around you. As you become more aware of your own social responsibility you try to minimise any harmful, or potentially harmful, effects of your actions or inaction. This is good citizenship and extends into areas such as:

* environmental protection, including energy-saving strategies, waste management and preservation of air quality

* health and hygiene at work, including personal cleanliness, public health regulations, employee healthcare policies and socially responsible travel

* the range of laws that apply in the workplace, including Health and Safety at Work (HASAWA) and the Provision and Use of Work Equipment Regulations (PUWER).

Proper disposal of waste on a building site is essential.

Environment issues in work

In this section you will learn about...

* **what the environment is, and how we can reduce our impact upon it**

* **waste disposal, reuse and recycling**

* **air quality and pollution**

* **public health policies.**

NAIL IT

Find out more about the atmosphere, climate and environment by visiting the following website:
www.ace.mmu.ac.uk/

Reuse – to use second-hand materials again without modifying them. Examples include old sinks, and reclaimed roof tiles and bricks, using the back of old reports or other paperwork for scrap paper, and refilling old printer cartridges.

Recycle – to use materials again, either for a different use from their original one, or by adapting or modifying the material. Examples include pulping old paper and cardboard to make new paper, and using old tyres to make a range of new objects.

In terms of workplace issues, the environment includes:

* the immediate area in which you work, including the air you breathe

* areas that may be joined to your work area by airflow or water flow

* the functioning of the natural systems of the planet Earth.

Environmental issues are those that:

* have a negative impact on the quality of air, water and soil, including:

    – burning rubbish on site that causes the emission of toxic gases

    – pouring hazardous chemicals, such as hydrochloric acid or caustic potash, down the drain

    – emptying oil or white spirits on to the soil.

* affect the systems and beauty of the natural surroundings, such as:

    – inefficient use of materials and lack of recycling, which leads to increased amounts of rubbish – where does it all go?

    – inefficient use of energy, causing unnecessary production of **greenhouse gases.**

Energy conservation and recycling

Much of the energy we produce involves burning fossil fuels such as oil, gas and coal. One of the by-products of this process is the production of substances that can harm the environment, such as greenhouse gases. Producing energy also costs money. Therefore by reducing the amount of energy we produce, we reduce the amount of harmful by-products and we save money. One way to cut down the amount of energy we use is to reduce the amount of energy we waste. This is called energy conservation. Wasting materials also costs money and increases the amount of rubbish for disposal. Over 100 millions tonnes of waste are disposed of in landfill sites in the UK each year. We can reduce the amount of rubbish produced by **recycling** or **reusing** materials, wherever possible, rather than simply throwing them away.

Reducing waste on building and construction sites results in reduced consumption of energy and resources, such as trees, oil and minerals used in the manufacture of construction materials.

The disposal of rubbish is a huge problem for a number of reasons. Crucially, in developed countries one of these is running out of space to bury or dispose of waste. Solutions include:

* being more efficient in the use of materials and wasting less

* using biodegradable materials

* increasing the use of reusable or recyclable materials.

Minimising the use of materials

The person on site responsible for ordering materials can minimise waste and expense by ensuring that:

* measurements are properly made

* materials are pre-cut to size

* there is only just enough of any one type of item for the job.

Staff must then make sure that these materials are stored and handled correctly so that none is wasted through being damaged. Damage to materials can occur if materials are stored in the wrong place, exposed to weather or incorrectly stacked.

Use of biodegradable materials

Biodegradable materials are those that completely decompose in landfill, forming part of the soil, or that can be composted. Natural organic materials are biodegradable – for example timber and paper, although treated materials, such as highly glazed paper or painted wood, can take longer to break down.

Reusable and recyclable materials

Some materials found on construction sites, and that used to be called waste, can actually be reused or recycled. They include:

* cardboard from packaging

* slate, tiles, timber and plasterboard:

  – offcuts of new materials or old materials removed before demolition or renovation

* old internal fixtures and fittings, such as cupboards, carpets and appliances

* metal pipes, ductwork and framing

* insulation

* bricks

* windows.

All of these materials are actually valuable and may be sold, recycled or reused.

DRILL DOWN

Can you find out some of the problems involved in disposal of waste through landfill? Search the internet using the terms 'landfill' and 'waste disposal'. Environmental charity sites and local authority sites have a lot of information on these topics. What alternative waste disposal methods are available?

NAIL IT

Find out more about waste minimisation in the construction industry by visiting the Scottish Environment Protection Agency website:
www.sepa.org.uk/wastemin/sector/construction.htm

NAIL IT

CIRIA is a company formed by a group of companies, universities and other interested organisations to research and promote best practice in the construction industry. One section of the website is devoted to construction waste and resources:
www.ciria.org/cwr/

TRY THIS

Think of one small project you could start, either by yourself or with your colleagues or family, which would help protect the environment. The project may take place at work, at college or at home, and may involve:

* reducing waste

* reducing energy use

* recycling materials.

The following websites may provide some ideas:

* Doing your bit – ways individuals can help the environment: www.doingyourbit.org.uk

* BBC education www.bbc.co.uk/learning/subjects/ environmental_studies.shtml

* The Council for Environmental Education: www.cee.org.uk

* Carymoor environmental education centre: www.carymoor.org.uk

* Environment agency: www.environment-agency.gov.uk

* Envirowise: www.envirowise.gov.uk

Note down what you plan to do and keep a record of your progress. Write a short report of the project after a period of time (negotiate this length of time with your teacher or trainer).

◨ Collecting and disposing of materials

The key to ensuring that you maximise reuse and recycling is to have an organised plan for the recovery, storage and disposal of these materials. This may involve having material-specific skips and containers on site: for example, one for bricks, one for timber and one for paper. This saves the time, money and energy that would be required to sort the materials. These can then be sent directly for reuse or recycling. The workforce should be encouraged to think of recycling or reusing materials, rather than just throwing them away. Construction companies should also ensure that any materials that cannot be reused or recycled are disposed of responsibly. Most local authorities have special facilities for the disposal of construction waste. This can cost money, so recycling and reusing as much as possible can also reduce these disposal costs.

case study

Bron, a demolition company manager, makes extra money by recycling some of the materials found on the demolition sites. The materials are removed with care and sorted into separate skips. Good quality building stone and bricks can be sold for up to £20 per tonne. Ordinary wood may fetch £300 per skip and floorboard joists in relatively good condition 15p per foot. 'Recycling makes good business sense,' says Bron. 'Why throw materials in the landfill if they are still worth money?'

Questions and activities

Discuss the following questions with your colleagues, teacher, supervisor or trainer:

1. What sort of materials would be reusable and recyclable from the demolition of a three-bedroomed Victorian house?

* If the financial return of doing this only broke even with the time and money expended on removing the materials would it still be worth doing? Can you identify any other benefits from recycling materials from the house?

* Make a list of the recyclable and reusable materials you could extract from an average house demolition.

2. Refer to the list of other recyclable material from the house discussed in question 1. For each type of material, or fixture or fitting, find out:

* where could these be sold?

* what sort of prices might the materials or items fetch?

* who might buy these materials?

EVIDENCE

Imagine a small construction project that you could undertake using mainly recycled materials (including fixtures and fittings). Make a rough plan of the project and estimate the type and amount of materials you would need.

1. Make a table listing:
   * each different type of material
   * where you could obtain the material
   * how much the material would cost.

Now, work out the total cost of the project.

2. Find out the total cost of the same project using new materials.

Cleaner environment

A clean environment is more pleasant to live and work in than an untidy or dirty one – but more importantly, it is also much safer and healthier. A clean and tidy work environment also gives an initial good impression of competence and professionalism to customers, clients and building and environmental inspectors.

⬛ Air quality and pollution levels

Air quality is adversely affected by traffic fumes and industrial processes. Toxic fumes and gases take up a much greater percentage of the air we breathe now than before industrialisation. However, legislation such as the Clean Air Acts in the UK and elsewhere in the 1950s, 60s and 70s have reduced the amount of pollution caused by industry and generally improved air quality. Even so, air pollution is still a problem, and there can also be local air pollution problems on construction sites. The main hazards on outdoor sites are dust and smoke, although legislation now places very strict limits on burning rubbish on site.

Dust containing asbestos or silica is extremely hazardous and can cause lung disease.

The issue of fresh air is even more important for people working inside, and especially for those working with chemicals and materials that give off potentially hazardous or toxic fumes and gas, such as solvents and adhesives. Internal workshops should have adequate ventilation and extraction equipment to ensure good air quality. This is in addition to the usual measures taken to protect staff from respiratory problems, such as the use of respirators and tools or equipment with dust bags or extractors attached.

⬛ Litter

Litter is not only unsightly, but also potentially dangerous, contributing to incidents and accidents such as fires, slips and falls. Legislation against littering means that it is an offence to drop waste on to the ground and leave it, under section 87 of the Environmental Protection Act 1990.

Common litter includes:

* cigarette ends – particularly dangerous if dropped when not put out

* packaging from sweets, snacks, cigarettes and take away meals

* used chewing gum

* food debris, for example unwanted lettuce out of a sandwich.

⬛ Waste disposal

All waste should be disposed of correctly – that is at the proper place, and in the correct type of container, if required. There is special legislation covering the disposal of hazardous substances such as oil, solvents and asbestos. These must be placed in suitable containers and collected by a licensed authority or disposed of at regulated sites.

Biodegradable waste produces methane gas, a **greenhouse gas** which contributes to the greenhouse effect, or **global warming**. It is more effective to

NAIL IT

The HSE publishes advice on dust control when using concrete cutting saws in the construction industry. Find out more on the following website: www.hse.gov.uk/pubns/cis54.pdf

Global warming – the rise in the overall temperature of the Earth's atmosphere and oceans due to heat from the sun being trapped by certain gases in the Earth's atmosphere.

Greenhouse gases – gases whose increased presence in the atmosphere has the effect of trapping the sun's heat, resulting in a rise in temperature of the Earth's oceans and atmosphere. The major greenhouse gases are carbon dioxide and methane.

dispose of biodegradable waste through composting than to send it to landfill. In fact, there a European Directive to reduce the overall amount of biodegradable waste placed in landfills each year.

WHAT WOULD YOU DO?

What if the government decided that there would be no waste or rubbish collections and no tips for dumping rubbish at all?

For one whole working day, make a list of all the materials that you dispose of, including:

* waste liquid poured down the sink or drain
* rubbish bagged up to go to the tip
* materials placed in skips
* everyday rubbish placed in bins at work or at home.

How much rubbish did you generate in just one day?

Organise your list into different types of waste and rubbish – for example, metal, plastic, paper etc. Then try to think of alternative ways that you could dispose of the rubbish. Remember – burning it is not an option.

NAIL IT

Find out more about the Landfill Directive at the Department for Environment, Food and Rural Affairs (Defra) website www.defra.gov.uk/environment/waste/topics/landfill-dir/index.htm

Find out more about waste disposal and sustainability on the atmosphere, climate and environment website: www.ace.mmu.ac.uk/eae/Sustainability/Older/Waste_Disposal.html

Health and hygiene relating to work

You have a personal responsibility to look after your own health as well as you can. This is just plain common sense, and yet many of us do things that we know are harmful to our health, such as smoking.

Public health policies in the workplace

There are several government public health policies and initiatives that are put in place to improve everyone's health or to increase safety, such as:

* **Anti-smoking regulations**

  – these regulations are under consultation in the UK and come into force in 2007 in England and Wales

  – this will mean that smoking is banned inside workplaces and public buildings.

* **Alcohol and drugs regulations**

  – employers are required, under the Health and Safety at Work etc. Act 1974, to ensure, as far as is reasonably practicable, the health, safety and welfare of employees

  – if an employer knowingly allows an employee to work under the influence of alcohol or drugs, and this causes an incident or accident, both the employer and employee could be prosecuted.

✳ **Lighting**

– the Workplace (Health, Safety and Welfare) Regulations 1992, Regulation 8(1) requires that every workplace has suitable and sufficient lighting.

✳ **Sun exposure** – excessive exposure to the sun can cause skin cancer – so if you are working outdoors in the construction industry you should take care to protect your skin by:

– always wearing a top – preferably with short sleeves to protect your shoulders

– wearing a hat which protects your forehead, ears and the back of your neck

– always using sunscreen with a protection factor above 15

– staying out of direct sunlight whenever you can – for example, during breaks.

EVIDENCE

Research one of the following topics with a small group of colleagues:

✳ anti-smoking regulations

✳ alcohol and drug testing at work.

Find out:

✳ what legal requirements exist

✳ what policies and procedures construction companies have in place

✳ how the employees feel about the law and the company policies and procedures.

Discuss the reasons why the laws and/or policies and procedures have been put in place. Do you agree or disagree with the reasons?

◪ Personal cleanliness

Personal cleanliness involves:

✳ daily bathing or showering

✳ regular hair washing

✳ twice daily teeth cleaning

✳ nail and hair cutting

✳ washing clothes

✳ washing hands, without fail:

– after visiting the toilet

– after working with toxic materials

– before preparing or eating food.

Hygiene and good grooming not only present a favourable impression on clients and the general public, but also help prevent:

* offensive body odour and halitosis (bad breath)
* the intake of toxins or germs when eating
* the transfer of disease.

General healthcare policies for employees

Some larger employers offer free or subsidised healthcare services, such as:

* employee assistance programmes (EAP) – provide counselling and support for all types of problems
* gym facilities
* health screening
* flu vaccination
* on-site nurse or other medical practitioner.

Private health insurance

In some companies, part of the pay package may include private health insurance, providing cover for the costs of optical, dental and other medical treatment.

Alternative methods of transport

There's no doubt that car exhaust fumes contribute to air pollution, but sometimes driving to work is the only option. However, you can investigate alternative transport methods which have a less damaging effect on the environment, for instance by reducing the use of petrol and the emissions from car exhausts. Examples include:

* car-pooling – where people who live near each other take it in turns, usually weekly, to drive the group to work
* using public transport, including:
  - trains
  - trams
  - underground or metro
  - buses.

Other initiatives to reduce the impact of traffic on the environment include:

* congestion charging in central London
* road pricing
* the use of alternative fuels, such as LPG, on public transport.

Most construction workers keep quite fit through their physical work, but you can increase fitness and health by walking or cycling to work.

The law

In this section you will learn about...

* what laws are and why they are there

* laws and regulations that affect you in the workplace.

Laws exist to help both you and your employer. They aim to enable society to manage all aspects of life fairly. The law is constantly revised and updated to take into account new situations and new technology.

How the law helps you at work

Many of the procedures, safe work methods or work instructions that you are given at work have some basis in the law. Workplace documents are designed to ensure that, if followed correctly, all work will be done according to legal requirements. Did you know that it's against the law to:

* refuse to give a person the correct wages

* tease a person at work

* work with hazardous equipment without protective clothing

* force a person to work long hours?

There are workplace policies and practices, also based on the law, ensuring that the employer provides all that is legally required for the employees.

Why do laws exist?

Laws make it quite clear what is right and what is wrong. Just like the rules of a game, the law tells you how to play fairly. There are laws about almost everything we do, covering two main areas:

* **criminal law** – dealing with crimes such as burglary, robbery and violence

* **civil law** – dealing with contract law, family law and property law.

How are laws made?

Laws are made, and changed, by Acts of Parliament. The government will consider and debate proposed new laws and changes to laws, and then vote on whether to accept them or not. When a law is accepted, the relevant government department has to put it into practice by making sure that everyone who needs to know about the law is well-informed. This usually means writing guidelines in plain English, as legal language can be very difficult to understand. For example, the Health and Safety Executive provides extensive on-line guidelines and advice on how to make sure that employers and employees know what to do to ensure that they follow health and safety law.

TRY THIS

Here is an example of legal language:

Extract from the Noise at Work regulations

'An employer who carries out work which is liable to expose any employees to noise at or above a lower exposure action value shall make a suitable and sufficient assessment of the risk from that noise to the health and safety of those employees, and the risk assessment shall identify the measures which need to be taken to meet the requirements of these Regulations.'

Can you rewrite this into plain English? Discuss it with your teacher or trainer.

NAIL IT

Find out what advice the HSE gives to employers who are trying to make sense of these regulations, by checking the website at the following address: http://www.hse.gov.uk/noise/advice.htm

Health and Safety at Work etc. Act

The Health and Safety at Work etc. Act covers both employer and employee responsibilities. Some general health aspects covered by this legislation include:

* ensuring workplaces where physical activities are performed are kept at a minimum temperature of 13°C

* provision of adequate lighting, especially for close detailed work, and in stairwells and passageways

* provision and use of personal protective equipment (PPE)

* working hours – no one should be expected to work more than 48 hours per week.

* breaks – most contracts of employment will specify what breaks you are allowed to take and whether you are paid for them. Breaks include tea breaks, lunch breaks and rest breaks – there are minimum break times set down in the working time regulations.

Provision and use of work equipment regulations (PUWER)

These regulations cover the suitability and use of equipment such as:

* hand tools

* ladders

* power tools

* lifting equipment

* plant (e.g. dumper trucks)

* motor vehicles.

Use of equipment can include any of the following activities:

* starting
* operating
* stopping
* cleaning
* maintaining
* repairing.

The employer must ensure that equipment either provided by them or brought into work by the employee is:

* suitable for the work to be done
* safe for use
* maintained in a safe condition
* used only by people who have received the proper instruction and training
* used in compliance with recommended safety measures such as protective equipment and warning notices.

Age restriction

The PUWER regulations limit the types of machinery that may be operated by young people under 18 years of age ('unless they have the necessary maturity and competence'). Machinery restricted to those over 18 years of age includes:

* power presses
* high-risk woodworking machinery, including:
    - all hand-fed woodworking machines
    - sawing machines fitted with a circular blade or saw band
    - planing machines used for surfacing
    - vertical spindle moulding machines.

For training purposes, people under 18 may operate this equipment under strict supervision.

Training requirements

Your employer needs to ensure that anyone using work equipment has received adequate training, instruction and information to operate that particular equipment safely. Training can be a simple matter of getting an experienced worker to show you what to do, or for more complicated equipment, completion of specific training courses.

Risk assessment

The management of Health and Safety at Work Regulations 1992 requires a risk assessment to be carried out on workplace equipment (Regulation 3(1)). The risk assessment should identify everything that should be done in order to ensure that equipment is safe and is used safely. The procedures or instructions for using the equipment will be based on the risk assessment and should be followed carefully.

case study

Adi is the Health and Safety Officer for a small construction firm involved in new-build housing projects. Adi knows from researching health and safety issues that 50 per cent of fatal accidents happen within the first week of a new worker starting on site. As Health and Safety Officer, Adi certainly doesn't want any injuries or fatalities on his conscience.

As each site has a different layout and design, Adi conducts a site safety induction for all workers. New starters stay on for an extra half hour so that Adi can check that all site safety issues are understood and answer questions. Topics include: risk assessments, safe work method statements, permits to work and electrical isolation.

Some of the new starters don't participate very much and don't ask any questions. Adi worries that these workers may not always be safe and responsible on site. He has to work out strategies to check that everyone is following safety procedures correctly.

Questions and activities

1. What questions might Adi expect to hear from the new workers starting on site?

2. What methods might Adi use to check that all safety procedures are followed correctly?

3. Research the safe work method statements for at least three tasks in your preferred area of work in the construction industry. Note down the name of the task, and the main points of the method statement, for each task.

4. What types of work require a 'permit to work'? Talk to experienced workers, or ask your supervisor to show you examples. List the information you would expect to find on a 'permit to work'

NAIL IT

Find out more about employment tribunals at www.employmenttribunals. gov.uk/

Other laws affecting you at work

There is other legislation that applies to all workplaces and which relates to rights such as privacy, equal opportunities, pay, conditions and confidentiality.

Equal opportunities legislation

This legislation prevents anyone discriminating against you – including not offering you a job – or treating you differently from others at work, based on your gender, race, religious faith or disability. If you think you have been treated unfairly on any of these grounds, you can appeal against decisions, or go to a third party, such as an employment tribunal, where the situation will be judged independently.

◘ Equal Pay Act

The Equal Pay Act ensures that people are paid at the same rate for the same or similar work; this includes basic pay, pension, sick and holiday pay, overtime and shift payments.

◘ Data protection

The Data Protection Act 1988 requires any company or organisation that holds personal information about a living person to ensure that the information is managed according to a set of eight principles. These state that personal information should be:

* processed fairly and lawfully

* obtained and used only for specified lawful purposes

* adequate and relevant for the purpose and not excessive

* accurate and, where necessary, kept up to date

* kept for no longer than necessary

* processed in accordance with the individual's rights

* kept secure

* transferred only to countries that offer adequate data protection and with the appropriate permission.

◘ Minimum pay

The National Minimum Wage is set by HM Revenue and Customs Department. There are three levels of minimum wage:

* a rate for workers aged 22 years and older (£5.35 per hour in October 2006)

* a development rate for workers aged from 18 to 21 years (£4.45 per hour in October 2006)

* a rate for all workers under the age of 18 who are no longer of compulsory school age (£3.30 per hour in October 2006).

Most apprentices are not covered by this legislation.

◘ Dangerous Substances and Explosive Atmospheres Regulations (DSEAR) 2002

These regulations outline the duty of employers to assess, and eliminate or control, the risk of fires and explosions from dangerous substances in the workplace. In the construction industry, dangerous substances may include acetylene gas, paint, aerosols and fuel.

◘ Transport legislation

There are several laws relating to transport. The main ones to consider in the construction industry are:

* The Road Safety Act 2006

* The Carriage of Dangerous Goods Regulations 2007.

NAIL IT

For more information about minimum wages, visit the HM Revenue and Customs website:
www.hmrc.gov.uk/nmw/

NAIL IT

For more information about the Dangerous Substances and Explosive Atmospheres Regulations, visit the HSE website at:
www.hse.gov.uk/fireand explosion/dsear/ background.htm

◘ The Clean Air Act

This legislation prevents the emission of dark smoke from any chimney or appliance. Several local authorities in the UK are designated Smoke Control Areas where no dark smoke is allowed.

WHAT WOULD YOU DO?

What would you do in each of the following circumstances?

1. You are paid the minimum wage, and the minimum wage is increased by the government, but there is no change in your pay packet.

2. A work colleague tells you to do a job that involves operating a machine you have never used before and have not received any training for.

3. You feel you are not being treated in the same way as other employees.

4. You are doing exactly the same job as another person in the company, but you find out that the person is paid more than you.

The following websites may be useful:

❋ The Citizenship Foundation: www.citizenshipfoundation.org.uk/

❋ The Commission for Racial Equality: www.cre.gov.uk/

❋ The Institute for Citizenship: www.citizen.org.uk/

5. If you could introduce one useful new law relevant to your workplace, what would it be?

EVIDENCE

Find out which laws apply to your most preferred career in the construction industry. List all the laws that apply, including those that apply to all workplaces. You may conduct your research by:

❋ talking to experienced workers

❋ interviewing company managers

❋ visiting advisory services

❋ searching the internet

❋ researching magazines and other recent publications.

Give a brief summary of how the law would apply to you when starting work in the construction industry.

Developing joinery skills

At the end of this unit you should be able to...

* recognise and select appropriate tools and personal protective equipment (PPE) to carry out simple joinery tasks

* apply safe working practices to the use of hand tools and equipment to produce simple joinery items

* apply safe working practices to the finish and preparation of joinery items to receive suitable applied finishes.

Unit overview

This unit introduces you to the commonly used hand tools, equipment and craft skills required to produce basic joinery items and prepare them to receive a suitable applied finish. Emphasis is placed on the correct selection and safe use of all hand tools, equipment and materials. You have the opportunity to develop an understanding of the principles, methods and safe working practices involved in the setting out, assembly and finishing of simple joinery items.

It is assumed that you will either have successfully completed Unit 3: Developing Skills and Working Safely in Construction before starting this unit, or that you will be studying Unit 3 alongside this unit.

This unit is internally assessed. This means, to pass you will complete a practical or written assignment set and marked by your tutor.

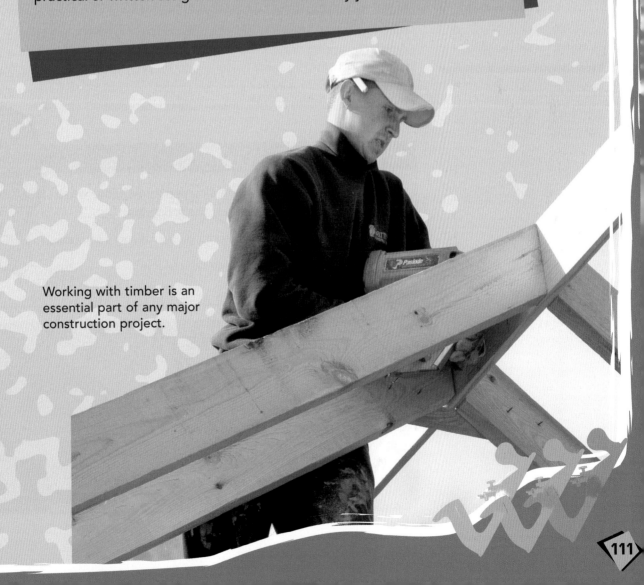

Working with timber is an essential part of any major construction project.

What is a carpenter and joiner?

In this section you will learn about...

* the work carried out by carpenters and joiners

* how to become a qualified carpenter or joiner.

Timber – wood prepared for carpentry or joinery.

Ironmongery – metal fitments to wooden structures, e.g. handles, bolts.

Partitions – floor to ceiling wood-framed panels used to divide up space inside buildings.

Carpenters and joiners are skilled operatives who work with **timber** and other related materials including plastic items and **ironmongery**. The carpenter's work is generally on-site fitting, fixing and installing timber items such as doors, windows, floors, roofs, stairs and **partitions**.

The joiner's work is mainly in the workshop, constructing timber items such as doors, door frames, windows and kitchen units, which a carpenter will then fit and fix into a building. A lot of carpenters and joiners these days can carry out both on-site and workshop work.

Carpenters and joiners must work to a high skills level to produce quality items of work. To be able to do this, all carpenters and joiners must be qualified to the necessary level. All newly qualified tradespeople will have followed and achieved an apprenticeship framework of qualifications which include a National/Scottish Vocational Qualification (N/SVQ) at Level 2 or Level 3, a Technical Certificate, Key Skills in Literacy and Numeracy and a health and safety test. To achieve Level 3 usually takes three years.

WHAT WOULD YOU DO?

Suppose you want to become a carpenter or joiner when you leave school. Try to answer the following;

* Who do you need to speak to for guidance and information?

* What questions would you need to ask them?

A joiner at work – note the PPE in use.

Hand tools, equipment and personal protective equipment (PPE)

In this section you will learn about...

* **different types of hand tools and equipment used by a carpenter and joiner**

* **how to use hand tools safely**

* **the correct PPE to use when using hand tools.**

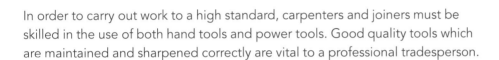

SAFE╋Y TIP

Before you study this section, make sure you have read Unit 3: *Developing skills and working safely in construction.*

In order to carry out work to a high standard, carpenters and joiners must be skilled in the use of both hand tools and power tools. Good quality tools which are maintained and sharpened correctly are vital to a professional tradesperson.

Hand tools

Although power tools are being used more and more in the industry, a carpenter and joiner will still need a wide variety of hand tools. There is a very wide range of tools available to the carpenter and joiner. Some of these are very specialist, so you are unlikely to come across them at this stage of your qualification. However, we will deal here with all the major hand tools that a qualified carpenter or joiner must have and be able to use correctly.

Tools can be classed as:

* tools that cut (e.g. saws and chisels)

* tools used for fixing items in place (e.g. screwdrivers)

* tools that plane and sand

* tools that bore or shape timber

* tools to assist the '**marking off**' process (e.g. rules)

* tools that clamp or hold timber in place.

We will now look at some hand tools that you will be learning how to use. You will also pick up some useful tips on how to stay safe when using the tools, and ideas to help your tools last longer.

SAFE╋Y TIP

It is extremely important that you and others stay safe when hand tools are being used. See the list of general safety guidelines on the use of hand tools on page 53.

Marking off – marking timber before cutting.

SAFE╋Y TIP

When using a hand saw it is important that when you start cutting you make the first cut by drawing the saw backwards. This stops the saw jumping off the mark and damaging your work or you!

Hand saws

There are five basic types of saws that a carpenter and joiner will use on a day-to-day basis. These are:

* rip saws

* cross-cut saws

Rip saw

* tenon saws
* dovetail saws
* coping saws.

Rip saw – usually used for cutting timber with the **grain**. The teeth of this saw are large and flat, shaped to cut like chisels. Each tooth is bent or set alternately to the right and to the left. This set prevents the saw blade jamming in the cut, or kerf, and also enables each tooth to cut easily. Most saw blades are also tapered in thickness from the tooth edge to the back for increased blade clearance and to stop it jamming.

Cross-cut saw – used to cut across the grain. The teeth of this saw are different from a rip saw. The teeth resemble knife points, each being sharpened at an angle across the blade to produce knife edges. When the saw is drawn across the wood it cuts two deep lines close together.

Tenon saw – specialist tools used for sawing **tenons** and small pieces of wood. The blade is short and of high-quality tool steel, hardened and spring-tempered all over. The teeth are similar in shape to those of a cross-cut saw, but smaller. The back of the saw is made of steel or brass and is fitted tightly to the back of the saw blade to hold it rigid. Brass backed saws are more expensive and are heavier than steel, and they do not rust. Steel backed saws are cheaper and strong, but tend to rust. The handle is made from hardwood and secured to the blade by means of brass screws and nuts.

Dovetail saw – specialist tool used for sawing **dovetails** and small accurate fine work. This saw is similar to the tenon saw but with smaller teeth. Its main purpose is for sawing along the grain for dovetailing. Some types have an open handle, others a closed handle.

Coping saw – used to cut along curved lines or for small work, and can cut with or against the grain. The frame of this saw is made of steel and the blade is kept in place by means of tension. The tension is created in the steel saw frame by turning a screw and bolt in the handle. The blade is very flexible and can be turned to any position. The teeth may be positioned to cut in any direction.

> **Grain** – the natural texture within a piece of timber – usually parallel with the direction in which the timber naturally splits.

> **Tenon** – a projecting piece of wood made to fit into a corresponding cavity to form a joint.
>
> **Dovetail** – similar to a tenon but smaller and tapered in shape like a fanned-out bird tail.

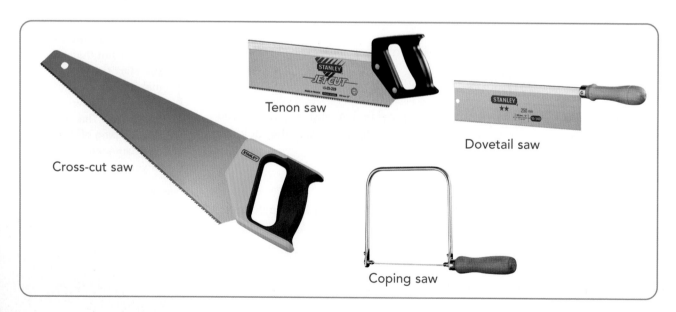

Cross-cut saw

Tenon saw

Dovetail saw

Coping saw

◖ Staying safe when using saws

Care should be taken when using saws. Incorrect use can often lead to nasty hand injuries. Here are some simple rules which can reduce the risk of injury.

* The timber should always be firmly supported.

* Always use the correct saw for the work in hand.

* Always use a saw that is sharp and with the correct tooth set.

* Never use a blunt or badly maintained saw.

* Never force the saw by applying too much force to the cutting stroke.

* Always use long cutting strokes so that all the teeth of the saw are being used.

* When nearing the end of the cut, saw lightly to avoid splintering.

* Make sure the work is securely clamped down before starting.

* Wear the correct PPE for the task, for instance safety glasses.

Bevelled-edge chisel

◖ Chisels

Chisels are available in a wide range and variety. Each one has a specific use. Below are the ones you are most likely to use. It is extremely important that chisels are kept sharp to ensure they carry out the job you want them to do. Never have any part of your body in front of the blade while you are using it. It is also important that you wear goggles if using a hammer or a mallet with a chisel.

Chisels have two main uses:

* cutting and shaping timber when a plane cannot be used

* cutting joints.

The size of a chisel is determined by the width of the blade. This varies from 2 mm to 50 mm but the most popular sizes range from 3 mm to 25 mm. The handles of chisels can be made from wood or plastic. Modern chisels have strong plastic handles which can withstand repeated blows from a mallet or hammer. These are the main chisels you will be using during your course.

Bevelled-edge chisel – has the back of the blade bevelled along both edges so that it can be used to cut in acute corners. It is a lightweight type of chisel suitable for **paring**. These chisels are available with wooden or plastic handles.

Firmer chisel – used for general bench and building site work. It is the strongest type of chisel. The blade is much stronger than a bevelled-edge chisel and can be used for paring or cutting joints. It can withstand light blows from a mallet, but care must be taken. If the chisel has a wooden handle it may split due to repeated blows from a mallet.

Mortise chisel – used for the cutting of mortises or slots, which often form part of a joint. This chisel is strongly made and is designed for heavy-duty work. The blade thickness prevents the chisel twisting in the mortise or slot.
The handle of this type of chisel can be wood or plastic and is stronger than other types of chisel. Some mortise chisels have a leather washer incorporated to absorb the shock when struck with a mallet or hammer.

> **Paring** – shaving down a piece of wood, taking off thin layers until the correct size and shape is reached.

Staying safe when using chisels

Care should be taken when using chisels. Incorrect use can often lead to nasty hand injuries. Here are some simple rules which can reduce the risk of such injuries.

* Always keep your hands behind the blade.

* Make sure you use the correct chisel for the job you are doing.

* Never point a chisel, or hand a chisel to someone blade first.

* Make sure the chisel is sharp at all times.

* Make sure all work is securely clamped down before starting.

* Wear the correct PPE for the task. This might include safety glasses or goggles.

Hammers

There are a number of hammers available to the carpenter and joiner in various weights and sizes. You will learn about a claw hammer, a pin hammer and a mallet. It is important you always wear goggles or protective safety glasses when using a hammer to protect your eyes from any flying shards.

Claw hammer – this is the most commonly used hammer. It is used to drive nails into timber and the claw can be used to extract bent or unwanted nails, which saves the carpenter from carrying pincers around. Claw hammers can have wooden shafts made from a hardwood like hickory or ash, or have shafts made from steel. It would mainly be used by building site carpenters

Pin hammer – this is the very smallest type of hammer, also known as a tack hammer. It is lighter than a claw hammer and has a cross pein instead of a claw. Hammer handles are usually made from ash or hickory. Pin hammers are used mainly by bench joiners.

Mallet – made from wood, usually beech, hickory or ash, and used to strike the handle of woodcutting chisels. The mallet has a much larger striking head than a hammer. The shaft of the mallet is tapered to make it self-tightening during use. When using a mallet, never strike the chisel with the side of the head, always use one of the two faces, otherwise the mallet will crack and break.

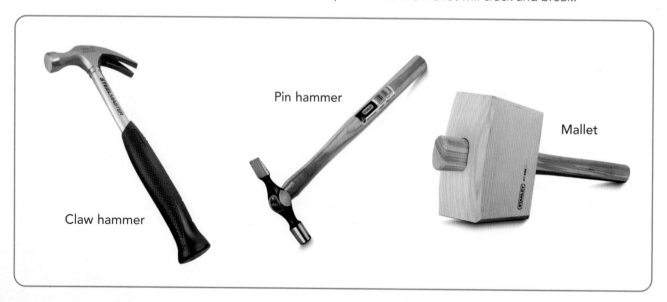

Pin hammer

Mallet

Claw hammer

Staying safe when using hammers

Care should be taken when using a hammer or mallet. Incorrect use can often lead to nasty injuries. Here are some simple rules which can reduce the risk of such injuries.

* Always wear goggles or safety glasses when using a hammer.
* Always keep hands well away from the impact area.
* Never hit a chisel with the side of a mallet.
* Wear the correct PPE for the task.

WHAT WOULD YOU DO?

You are using a mallet and a crack appears on the shaft. What would you do?

Screwdrivers

The type and size of screwdriver used should relate to:

* the type and size of screw
* the speed required to insert the screw fully
* the position and location of the screw
* the quality of the finished work.

There are three basic types of hand-driven screwdrivers which are of use to the carpenter and joiner.

Fixed blade screwdriver – a normal screwdriver with a wooden or plastic handle.

Ratchet screwdriver – this has a ratchet mechanism in the handle which means it turns freely in one direction, without turning the blade, but is fixed in the other direction like a normal screwdriver. The direction can be reversed. Screws can be screwed in (or taken out) with a ratchet screwdriver without having to change your grip on the handle.

Spiral screwdriver – also called a pump-action screwdriver. It has a mechanism in the handle which means that when you apply downward pressure to the handle the blade is forced round. You effectively pump up and down to turn it, rather than twisting it.

Fixed blade slotted screwdriver

Ratchet screwdriver

SAFETY TIP

A screwdriver can be as dangerous as a chisel. Always keep your hands behind the point where you are using it.

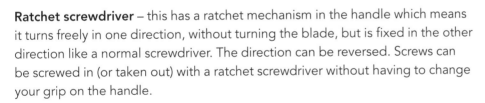

Spiral or pump-action screwdriver

The most common types of screwdriver head are:

* **slotted head** – for screws with a conventional single groove across the head.

* **Phillips® cross-head** – for screws with a cross-groove that can only be fitted by Phillips® screwdrivers.

* **Pozidriv®** – for screws with a cross-groove and a square hole in the centre that can only be fitted by Pozidriv® screwdrivers.

Planes and sanding methods

There are many types of planes available today. All of them are capable of cutting wood, but not all are designed to plane wood to a flat surface. Each type of plane has its own function and use, and the shape of the blade is designed to carry out a specific task. It is important when a plane is not in use that it is laid on its side so as not to damage or blunt the blade.

Planes can be divided into two main types:

* bench planes

* special purpose planes.

At this stage of your course you will probably only be learning about bench planes. The two main types are a jack plane and a smoothing plane. Both are designed to plane flat surfaces on timber.

Jack plane

Jack plane – has a relatively long blade to allow for rapid removal of waste material from larger jobs. Surfaces left by the jack plane are not regarded as finished. Further planing with a smoothing plane will follow to bring your work to its finished quality.

Bevelling – creating a sloping edge.

Chamfering – bevelling a corner with an equal amount removed from each face.

Smoothing plane – this is shorter in length than a jack plane and is used for final finishing or cleaning up your finished job. The plane blade is ground and sharpened, with corners slightly rounded. It can also be used for **bevelling** or **chamfering**. This plane is capable of taking off very thin shavings from all over the surface of the timber. The purpose of this is to leave the finished timber clean and smooth with no previous plane marks showing.

Sandpaper and block – this is is the simplest sort of sander to use. Wrap a piece of the required grade of sandpaper around a solid block, such as a piece of wood. This gives you something solid to hold when sanding down a piece of work. This is sufficient for rough sanding. For finer sanding you would use sandpaper without the block.

Smoothing plane

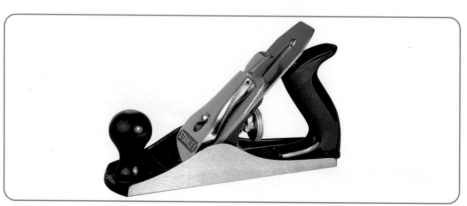

◎ Staying safe when using planes

Planes are quite heavy tools. Be sure they are left in a safe position so they do not fall off a bench on to your feet. Plane blades are sharp, so always treat them with respect. Make sure you retract the blades when not in use. Always use the correct PPE: this might include safety glasses or goggles.

◎ Tools for boring

The making of a hole in timber is known as boring. It is best to attempt boring either horizontally and vertically, rather than at an angle. There are many reasons why carpenters and joiners need to insert holes into timber, for instance to insert a screw or to allow for the fitting of ironmongery. Many of these tasks have now been taken over by power tools, but it is still important that a carpenter and joiner can use all hand-boring tools expertly.

Bradawl – used to make small pilot holes in timber to insert a screw or to provide a centre mark for drilling. The bradawl has a sharp point and should be pushed into the timber, not hit with a hammer.

Ratchet brace – a very useful and versatile tool, which can be used anywhere since it does not rely on electricity to power it. The brace relies solely on applied pressure and the turning of a handle. The ratchet brace is usually fitted with universal jaws. The jaws are contained in a chuck shell, which is screwed to the frame of the brace. The jaws grip the different sizes and types of drill bit that can be used with the brace.

Wheel brace – used to hold straight-shank twist drills. It is a handy tool for the accurate drilling of small holes in timber. It is very light and portable and can be used when no power tools are available. The chuck is turned by means of the small hand wheel, which can be difficult when drilling hard or dense material.

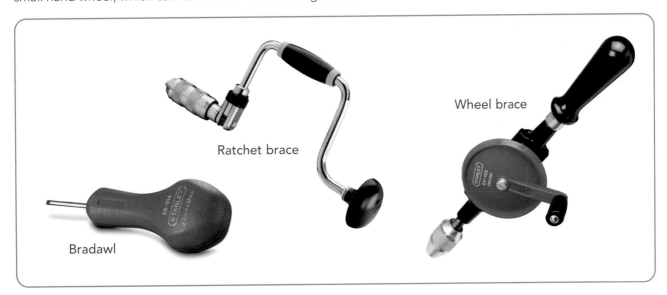

Ratchet brace

Wheel brace

Bradawl

◎ Staying safe when using tools for boring

Drill bits can be sharp and also heat up when in use, so do not touch the cutting parts of a drill bit. Be careful when handling sharp implements such as bradawls, and protect the tip with a cork or other protector. Carry them by the point, not the handle, so that if you trip or fall with one, you are less likely to harm yourself, or someone else, with it. Depending on what you are drilling, you may be required to wear safety glasses or goggles and a face mask so you don't inhale fine material produced by the drilling.

Measuring and marking-out tools

Measuring tools are used either to transfer measurements from one component to another or to check known measurements. Accuracy is all-important when either transferring or checking measurements, as any mistakes could cost you, or your employer, a lot of money and wasted time.

Remember: **Measure twice cut once!**

The main tools used for measuring and marking out are:

* pencil
* rules and measures – folding rule, steel rule, steel tape measure
* squares – tri-square, mitre square, combination square
* sliding bevel
* gauges – marking gauge, mortise gauge.

Pencils – these are graded by the hardness of the lead. A good pencil to use for carpentry and joinery work is 2H. This is quite hard and gives an accurate line. It is extremely important to keep your pencils sharp so that any measurements you mark with it are accurate and clear.

Folding rule – this is one of the most important measuring tools. It is available in both wood and plastic, and includes both imperial and metric measurements. With care these rules will last for many years, but excessive bending and twisting can lead to breakage.

Steel rule – used for fine accurate work and comes with both metric and imperial measurements. These are mainly used by bench joiners for setting out in a workshop. They are durable, and the metal edge is less easy to damage than a plastic one so will provide an accurate straight edge when drawn against.

Steel tape measure – this is made of thin steel with metric or a combination of imperial and metric measurements. These tapes retract on to a small enclosed spring-loaded drum and are pulled out and pushed back into the housing. Some have an automatic return, which can be stopped at any distance within the limit of the tape's length. They are used for setting out large areas and have a hook at the end so the tape can be held over the edges of the material being measured. The length of these tapes can vary from 2 m to 8 m.

Folding rule, steel rule and steel tape measure

Squares

Tri-square – this is used to mark out and test pieces of timber for squareness and to ensure they are at 90 degrees. The tool is made of hardwood, which is faced with a brass plate, and a steel blade, which is fixed at right angles to the stock at one corner. It should be regularly checked for accuracy.

Mitre square – this consists of a blade fixed at 45 degrees secured to a hardwood handle. This square is used mainly to mark off mitres or lines at 45 degrees.

Combination square – this does the job of both the mitre and tri-square. Some versions of this square also have a spirit level in-built into the handle.

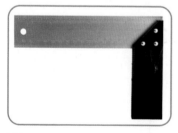

Tri-square

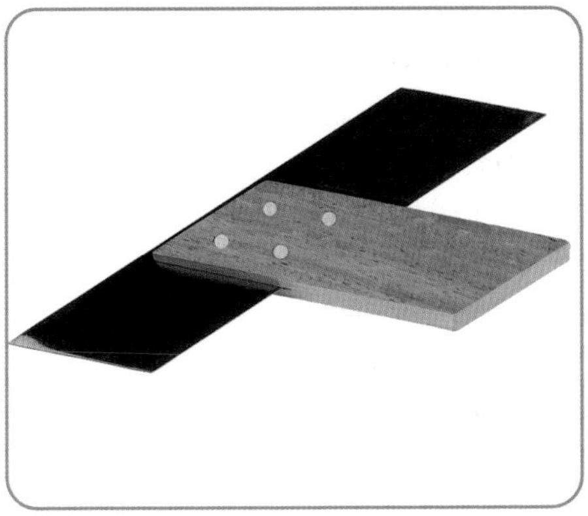

Mitre square

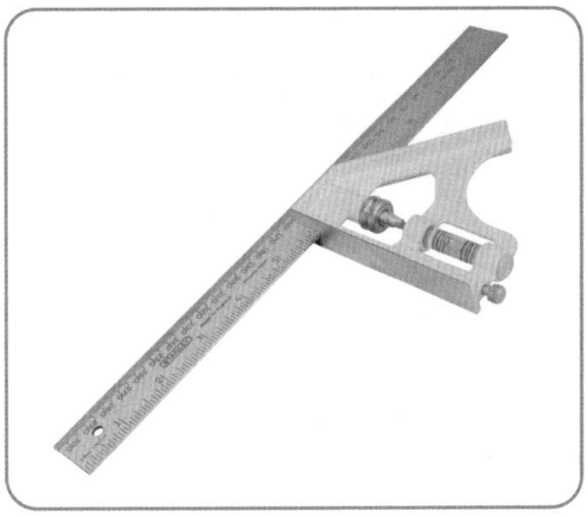

Combination square

Sliding bevel

A sliding bevel can be adjusted to any angle as the blade slides within the handle. It can be locked at any angle and is very useful when acute angles have to be marked.

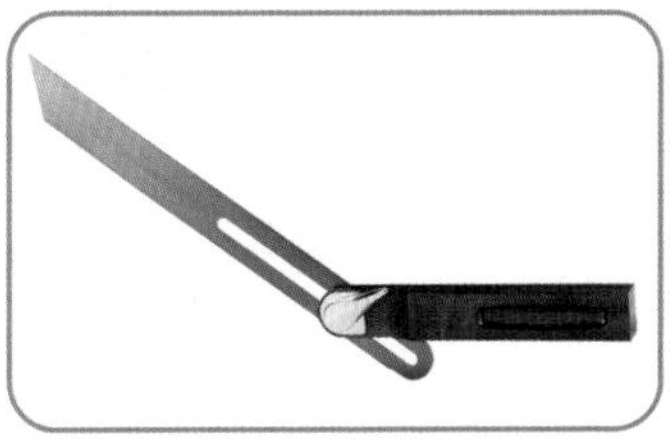

Sliding bevel

Gauges

Marking gauge – this is used to score a single line parallel to the edge of a piece of timber. It has brass inserts in the handle to reduce wear and tear.

Mortise gauge – this is similar to the marking gauge except that it has two adjustable parallel marking spurs. One of the spurs is fixed to the stem, and the other is fixed to a brass slide housed in the stem. The slide can be adjusted by a thumb screw. The main use of this gauge is to mark the position of mortises and tenons. It is possible to buy a gauge that is a combination of a marking gauge and a mortise gauge.

Marking gauge

Mortise gauge

Clamps

Carpenters and joiners often need to grip their work or hold it to a bench. Clamping tools are usually designed to meet a particular need for a specific job or process, and it is important to use the correct clamp for the job you are carrying out.

G-cramps – available in several sizes and depths. These clamps can be very useful in applying a lot of pressure to two different items. It is important to always protect your work from the pressure points of the clamp with scrap pieces of timber. Some G-cramps now have a quick release mechanism to allow them to be used more efficiently.

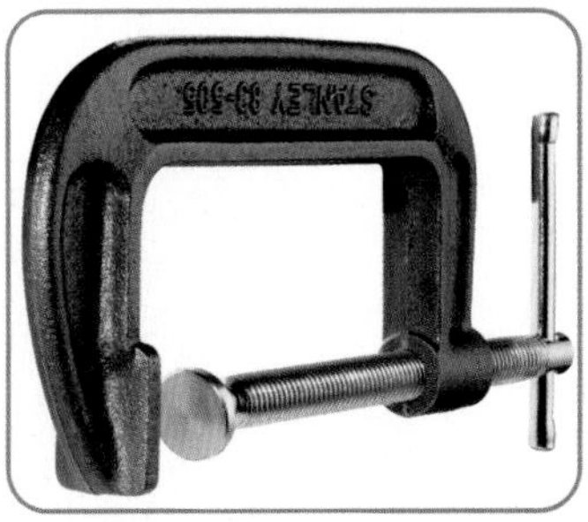

G-cramp

Sash clamps – so called because of their original use in clamping together components of windows and door frames. They are normally used in pairs. They are also extremely useful for carrying out other workshop jobs that are too big for G-cramps. The sash clamp is locked in place with a pin, and pressure is applied by turning the handle.

Bench hook – designed to fit into a vice on the joiners' bench. The bench hook is designed to rest the workpiece against when sawing short lengths of timber.

Sash clamp

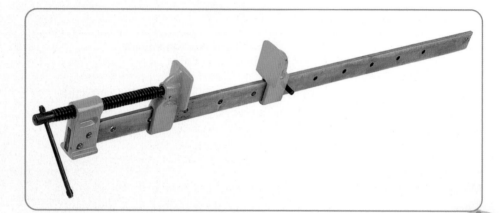

TRY THIS

Name the correct tools to carry out these jobs.

* Marking out a mortise and tenon joint.

* Chopping out a mortise.

* Cutting a curved line on a piece of plywood.

* Making a small pilot hole in timber before inserting a screw.

* Cutting across the grain of the timber.

Personal protective equipment

Along with other workers on a construction site, you will be required to wear the appropriate PPE. Depending on the site and the job you are doing, this might include:

* hard hat

* reflective jacket

* steel-toed boots

* overalls

* eye protection

* ear protection

* gloves.

You should wear the appropriate PPE as directed by your supervisor.

Timber

In this section you will learn about...

❋ **the difference between hardwood and softwood**

❋ **the different qualities of timber**

❋ **how timber is converted to be used by a carpenter and joiner**

❋ **how timber is seasoned.**

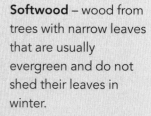

Softwood – wood from trees with narrow leaves that are usually evergreen and do not shed their leaves in winter.

Hardwood – wood from trees with broad leaves that are deciduous and lose their leaves in winter.

Hardwood and softwood

Timber is classified either as **softwood** or **hardwood**. Don't get confused, as not all hardwoods are hard and not all softwoods are soft! The terms refer to the type of tree the timber comes from and not to the actual strength of the timber.

◪ Softwoods

Softwoods are timbers from trees such as the pine, fir, spruce and larch. These trees are known as conifers because their seeds are enclosed in cones. They have long, hard, needle-like, green leaves, each of which lives four or five years. The needles are replaced a few at a time, and don't all fall at once, so the trees always appear green. For this reason they are often called **evergreens**. Larch is an exception as it loses its needles every year. The structure of softwood timber is simple and the wood is usually **resinous**, soft and easy to work with, although some softwoods, such as yew, are quite hard.

Evergreen – trees that *do not* lose their leaves in winter. Most conifers are evergreen.

Resinous – containing resin – a strong-smelling, sticky substance in the wood.

Deciduous – trees that *do* lose their leaves in winter. Common trees such as oak, ash and beech are deciduous.

TRY THIS

How many hardwoods and softwoods you can name from memory? When you have completed this, carry out some research and see how many more you can find.

◪ Hardwoods

These come from trees that have broad leaves such as oak, ash, beech and mahogany. They are known as **deciduous** trees because they shed their leaves in the autumn. Hardwood timbers often have a more complex structure than softwoods.

DR LL DOWN

A tree is generally regarded as consisting of five main parts – can you find out what these parts are? Which parts can provide usable timber?

Qualities of timber

Wood is a very versatile material. It is:

❋ relatively light and strong

❋ pleasant to touch and look at

❋ easily cut, shaped and joined

* capable of being fastened with glue, nails and screws
* capable of being finished in a variety of ways, such as by painting, varnishing or polishing.

Different timbers vary in their physical properties, for instance:

* weight
* colour
* durability
* grain
* strength
* smell.

◙ Qualities of softwood

Softwood is in great demand for building work such as roofs, staircases, floors and general construction work. It is used in much greater quantities than the harder, heavier and more expensive hardwoods. Its normally simple, straight grain makes it easy to cut, and it is of equal strength along its length. It comes from relatively fast-growing trees, which are easy to 'farm' in managed forests. It is often cheaper than hardwoods.

◙ Qualities of hardwood

Hardwood tends to be used for high-class interior joinery work and furniture-making. Many hardwoods have an attractive colour or distinctive grain that make them sought-after for decorative items, such as furniture and panelling. Hardwoods tend to be more expensive than softwoods.

Timber conversion

Timber conversion means sawing a log into boards or planks ready to be used by the carpenter or joiner. After felling, the log is cut into convenient lengths and sizes so it can be easily dried and **seasoned**. The way the log is cut will depend upon several factors, for instance the size, type and condition of the log and the size and type of sawing machine.

> **Season** – the controlled drying of green timber before it is used.

There are four main methods of conversion:

* through and through
* quarter
* tangential
* boxed heart.

◙ Through and through

The simplest way of converting a log is to saw it into parallel boards. This is called 'plain through and through' or 'flat sawing'. It is a quick, cheap method of converting timber.

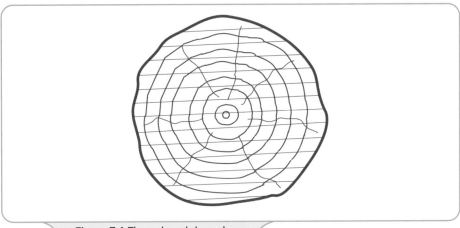

Figure 7.1 Through and through conversion

Quarter sawn

In this method the log is cut into quarters, and all other cuts are kept radially on the line of the rays as far as possible. This method of conversion produces hard-wearing surfaces suitable for flooring, and boards that keep their shape much better, and shrink less, than plain-sawn boards.

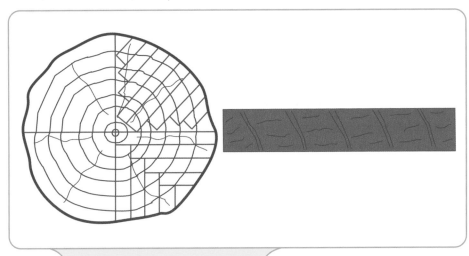

Figure 7.2 Quarter sawn conversion

Tangential sawn

Tangential sawn conversion is used to produce floor joists and beams as it gives the strongest timber. The log is cut along four sides at a tangent to the growing rings.

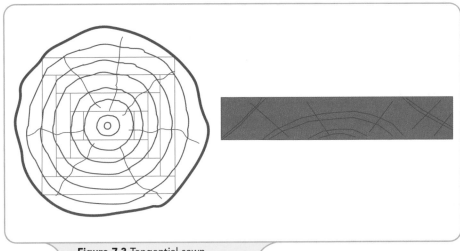

Figure 7.3 Tangential sawn conversion

◙ Boxed heart sawn

This is used when the **heart** of the tree is rotten or damaged. Timber produced using this method is often used for floor boards as it is hard-wearing and does not distort.

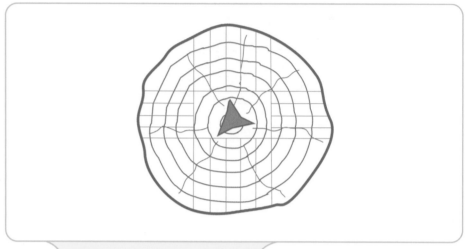

Figure 7.4 Boxed heart sawn

Drying and seasoning of timber

When a tree is felled, more than half of its weight consists water or 'moisture'. Freshly felled timber is called 'green timber'. It is almost unusable as it shrinks and often warps as it dries, so any measurements and joints made when the timber is green are likely to change and warp as the wood dries. Green timber is also very difficult to cut and work with.

To make the timber more stable and suitable for use, the excess water within the timber has to be reduced. But this must be done carefully, as uncontrolled removal of the water will cause shrinkage and distortion. The controlled removal of water is called seasoning.

There are two main methods of seasoning timber:

* natural – called air seasoning
* artificial – normally called kiln seasoning.

Timber being seasoned

Simple joinery items

In this section you will learn about...

* simple woodworking joints

* 'setting out' before starting to cut joints

* making frames

* health and safety.

Simple joints

Joiners usually join pieces of timber together by using woodworking joints. These joints make the job stronger and do not show any fixings, such as nails or screws.

Dovetail joint

These joints are a **housing** joint mainly used in the manufacture of drawers or boxes. The wedge shape of the dovetail stops the joint being forced apart.

> **Housing joint** – a joint where a slot is created in one piece of wood to house an equivalent shape in the joining piece of wood.

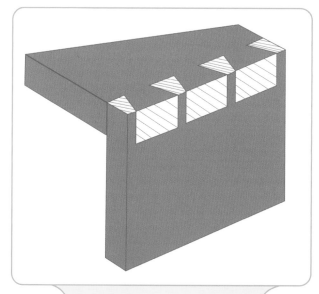

Figure 7.5 Through dovetail joint

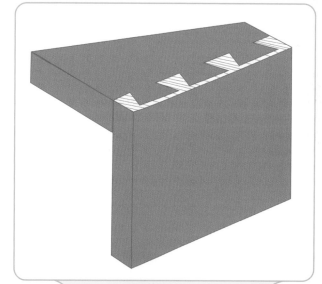

Figure 7.6 Lapped dovetail joint

Mortise and tenon joints

Mortise and tenon joints come in a variety of forms and are mainly used in the manufacture of doors and windows. There are five main types:

* through

* stub

* haunched

* twin

* double.

Through – a single tenon is slotted into a mortise that goes all the way through the piece of wood being jointed.

Stub – the tenon is cut short and the mortise is not cut completely through the member so that the tenon does not protrude through the member.

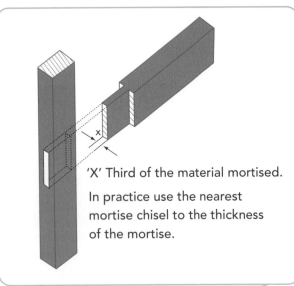

'X' Third of the material mortised.

In practice use the nearest mortise chisel to the thickness of the mortise.

Figure 7.7 Through mortise and tenon joint

Shortened tenon

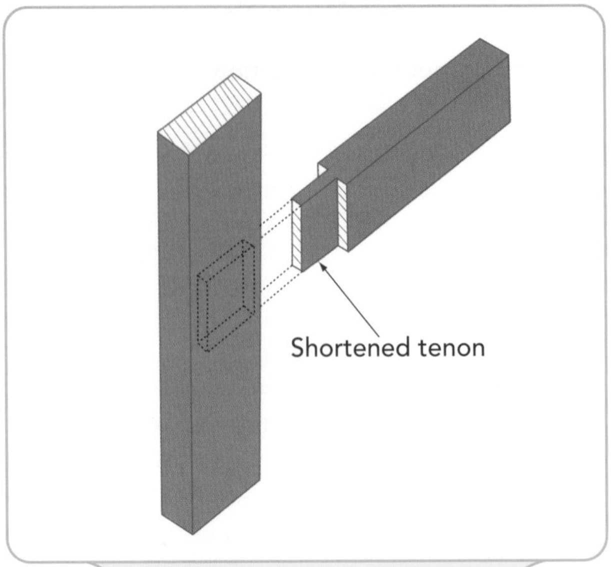

Figure 7.8 Stub mortise and tenon joint

Haunched – very similar to a through or stub mortise or tenon joint, except that a section (usually a third) of the tenon is removed to create a haunch. The purpose of this is to prevent the joint twisting.

Twin – a haunch is cut into a wide tenon at top and bottom, creating two tenons, one above the other.

Double – two tenons (and equivalent mortises) are created side by side in the timber. This makes for a very strong joint.

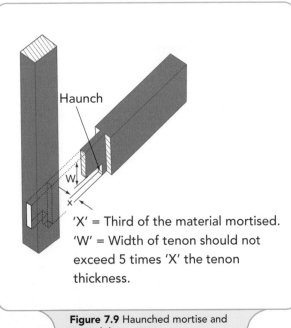

Haunch

'X' = Third of the material mortised.
'W' = Width of tenon should not exceed 5 times 'X' the tenon thickness.

Figure 7.9 Haunched mortise and tenon joint

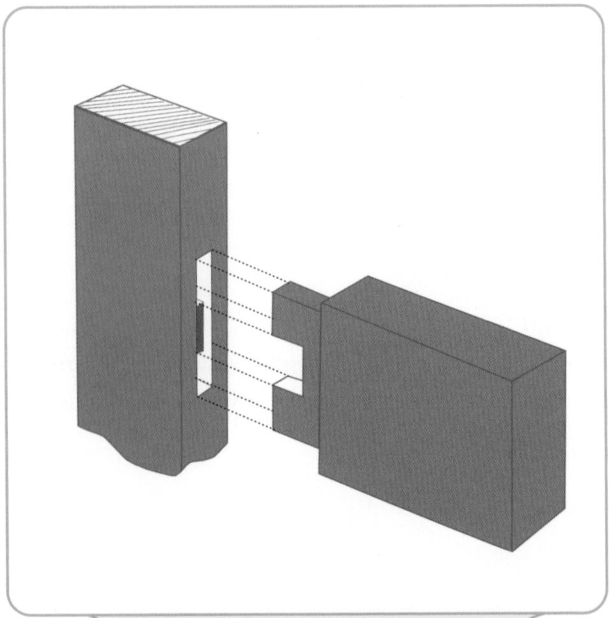

Figure 7.10 Twin mortise and tenon joint

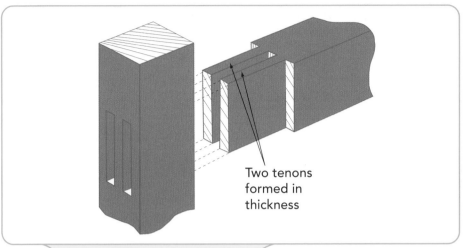

Figure 7.11 Double mortise and tenon joint

Two tenons formed in thickness

Halving joints

These are simple joints used to either lengthen timber or join it at a 90-degree angle. They are formed by removing the same amount from each piece of timber so that when they are fixed together, the joined section is the same width as the unjoined section. There are several methods of halving.

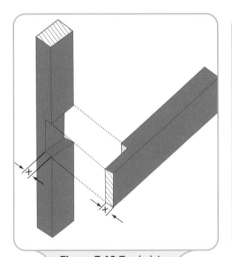

Figure 7.12 Tee halving or half lap joint

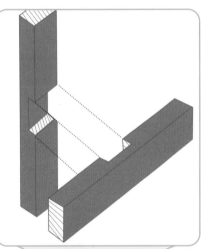

Figure 7.13 Cross halving joint

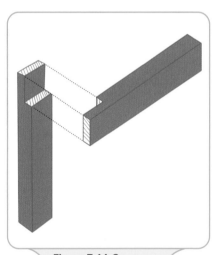

Figure 7.14 Corner halving joint

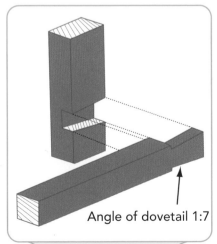

Angle of dovetail 1:7

Figure 7.15 Dovetail halving joint

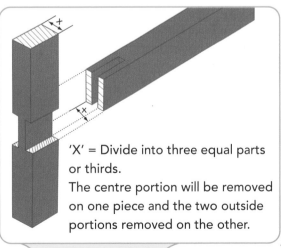

'X' = Divide into three equal parts or thirds.
The centre portion will be removed on one piece and the two outside portions removed on the other.

Figure 7.16 Tee bridle joint

Setting out

Setting out is the term used to describe the process of marking off the components of a joinery item. The process of setting out translates measurements, details and specifications from a drawing, or from written or verbal instructions, to the materials that are then used to construct the joinery item in question.

Setting out rod

No matter how small or simple the joinery item may be, it is always good practice to set out the components using a 'workshop' or 'setting out' rod.

This is a full-size drawing of the vertical and horizontal elevations of the joinery item. It will show all the dimensions and components of the item, and where and how they are incorporated in the finished product.

Rods are usually drawn on hardboard, thin plywood or other types of sheeting, such as MDF (Medium Density Fibreboard). The sheet is painted white to show the marking off more clearly. You can use paper, but this often tears or becomes unreadable due to inevitable creasing and folding, and is therefore not always recommended. However, it does have the advantage of being more easily stored for future use than timber sheets.

A setting out rod should contain the following information:

* all sizes and dimensions related to the item and its components

* the size, position and type of the joints

* the rod number, if it has one

* the contract number if it has one

* the number of the drawing the rod relates to

* the date it was drawn and by whom

* the number of items required from the rod.

You will need the following tools for setting out joinery items:

* rule or tape for measuring

* hard pencil (2H)

* marking and mortise gauges for gauging joints and rebates

* bevel for marking angles

* tri-square or combination square for marking off lines square or at right angles

* dividers for spacing off components and curves.

TRY THIS

Preparation is everything in carpentry and joinery; if you don't get the dimensions right in the first place, the job will be ruined. Bearing this in mind:

* List the advantages of using a workshop rod.

* State the purpose of setting out.

Contract No.							
Job Description: No 6 Traditional casement windows with one opening sash							
Item	**No. Req.**	**Length**	**Sawn sizes**		**Finished sizes**		**Material**
			Width	Thickness	Width	Thickness	
Jambs	8	900 mm	100 mm	75 mm	95 mm	70 mm	Softwood
Heads	4	600 mm	100 mm	75 mm	95 mm	70 mm	Softwood
Sills	4	600 mm	150 mm	75 mm	145mm	70 mm	Hardwood
Sash stiles	8	850 mm	50 mm	50 mm	45 mm	45 mm	Softwood
Sash toprails	4	550 mm	50 mm	50 mm	45 mm	45 mm	Softwood
Sash sills	4	550 mm	75 mm	50 mm	70 mm	45 mm	Softwood

Figure 7.17 Cutting list

Cutting lists

After the workshop rod has been completed a cutting list can then be compiled. This is a list of all the material required for a particular item of joinery. The list

enables timber to be ordered and prepared for the required job. All the information required to complete a cutting list is acquired from a workshop rod. There are many different designs and layouts for cutting lists, but the one given below shows all the information required to complete the marking off and assembly process for a casement window.

TRY THIS

Ask your tutor to give you an example of a joinery item, such as a frame, which needs to be constructed. Complete a cutting list for it accurately allowing for the minimum waste.

Marking out

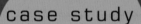 Marking out

All timber for the given job should be marked from your workshop rod. It is extremely important before you start marking out that you check over your workshop rod once again for accuracy. The marking out process should be as clear and as simple as possible with no unnecessary lines. You should always use a sharp and hard pencil.

Identifying the face and edge of the timber is very important. These will be the two best adjacent sides of the timber. You will need to check each face and edge on the timber and look for any defects that might affect the finish of your job and the cutting of joints, bevels and rebates. Your chosen face and edge will usually have the fewest defects. All marking out and measurements will be taken from your face and edge.

It is also good practice to mark out identical items together by laying them side-by-side and marking out across all items in one go.

case study

Sandeep works for a medium-sized joinery firm that has a contract to produce 500 window frames for houses on a new building site. He has been told to do the workshop rod for the bathroom windows (50 windows in all). He is given the architect's plans to draw the rod from. Other workers in the company will then make up the windows from his rod. After the windows are delivered to site it is discovered they are all the wrong size.

Questions and activities

1. List the problems this will give.

2. Why do you think the windows were the wrong size? List as many places as you can in the process where errors could have been made.

3. If you had been given Sandeep's job, describe how you would have made the workshop rod.

Making a frame

You should always follow the procedure below when assembling a frame. It is extremely important that you sand down the inside edges of your frame before assembly, as this will prove difficult when your frame is assembled.

❋ **Dry assembly**

After finishing cutting your joints you should try putting them together to see if they fit correctly. When each individual joint fits you should then try assembling the full frame with no adhesive to ensure all joints fit and that your frame is not twisted (winding). Depending on the job, your frame might use housing, through or mortise and tenon joints. If there are any problems, this is the stage to correct them.

❋ **Winding in**

Winding means twisted. You should use winding rods to check your frame to see if it is twisted. To do this you need to use two identical pieces of timber, which you should lie parallel on top of your frame while it is lying flat on the workbench. Close one eye and look over the top of the winding rods: they should be parallel. If they are, the frame is not twisted. If they are not parallel, you will need to make amendments to one or more of your joints. This all has to be done before you assemble the frame with adhesive.

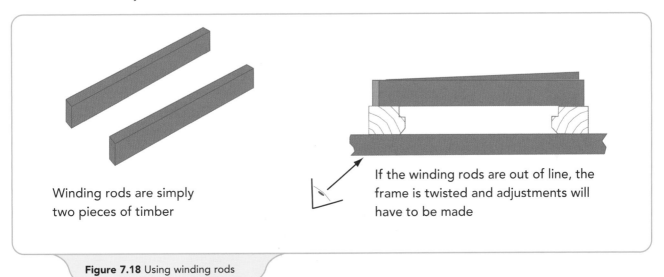

Winding rods are simply two pieces of timber

If the winding rods are out of line, the frame is twisted and adjustments will have to be made

Figure 7.18 Using winding rods

❋ **Squaring-up**

If you are happy after the dry assembly stage you should then fit your frame together using the appropriate adhesive. Your frame should be held together using clamps, and you should test the frame while still wet to ensure it is square (corners are at right angles). You should then use a squaring rod to compare the diagonals of the frame. The rod is a rectangular piece of timber with a small pin or nail protruding from it. The nail is placed in one corner of the frame and the rod positioned diagonally across the frame to the opposite corner.

Mark with a pencil the opposite diagonal on to the rod. Repeat this on the other diagonals. If both pencil marks line up, your frame is square; if not, you will need to make slight adjustments by realigning the clamps and moving the frame. You should repeat the squaring-up process until the pencil marks line up.

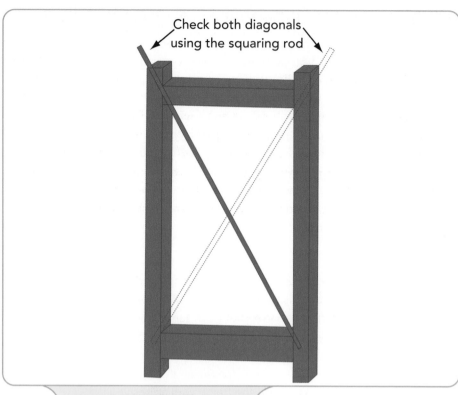

Figure 7.19 Squaring up

✳ Wedging Up

Wedging up is only necessary on mortise and tenon joints. This should be done after the frame has been dry assembled, squared up, checked for winding and glued. Wedging involves placing a small timber wedge on either side of the tenon by carefully driving it in to ensure the joints are tight. It's always best to insert the external wedges first.

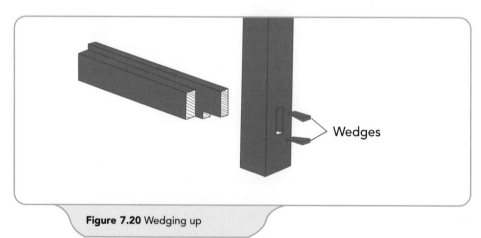

Figure 7.20 Wedging up

▣ Estimates and quantities

Carpenters and joiners must possess good skills in calculation and measurement for two main reasons:

* ✳ to give people a price to undertake work

* ✳ to be able to measure and estimate correctly.

In the construction industry the main measurements used will be millimetres and metres. Occasionally inches and feet are used, but never centimetres.

EVIDENCE

Make and assemble a frame

You can choose which joints you wish to use to assemble the following frame. The more complex the joint completed to a good standard, the higher your finished mark will be. Remember, though, a simple joint completed to a good quality finish is better than a complex joint finished to poor quality. Your teacher or tutor will help and advise you which joints they feel will be best for you to use. Look at the marking schedule in the appendix at the back of this book, as it will give you guidance on the standards you are expected to work to.

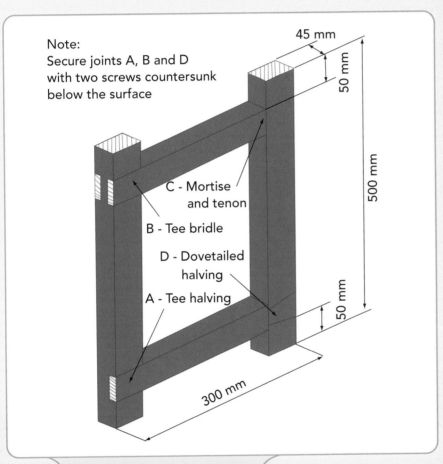

Note:
Secure joints A, B and D
with two screws countersunk
below the surface

45 mm

50 mm

500 mm

C - Mortise
and tenon

B - Tee bridle

D - Dovetailed
halving

A - Tee halving

50 mm

300 mm

Figure 7.21 Frame to be assembled

TRY THIS

For the frame in the Evidence Activity above, work out how much timber you will need for 25 frames. Add on 5 per cent extra for waste.

Work out how much it will cost for the timber for the 25 frames if the timber costs 65 pence a metre. Also add on 17.5 per cent VAT.

Health and safety

You will have seen in the tool sections how to work safely with the day-to-day tools and equipment you will use as a joiner or carpenter. You should also be aware of how to work safely when undertaking carpentry and joinery tasks. Following these simple guidelines should help you:

* Identify any hazards before starting a job.

* Report any hazards or damaged equipment.

* Do not fool around in the workplace.

* Wear the correct PPE.

* Maintain a clean and tidy workspace.

* Use the right tool for the job.

* Keep tools with blades properly sharpened and protect the blades when not in use.

At each stage of this unit you will be set practical tasks that will be assessed by your teacher or tutor. It is very important that you have been working on Unit 3 so that you have knowledge of health and safety when carrying out these tasks in the workshop. Your tutor should also demonstrate how to safely use the hand tools and how best to plan and carry out your tasks. If you are unsure about anything relating to health and safety, ASK!

Suitable timber finishes

In this section you will learn about...

* **creating a finish with a plane**

* **creating a finish with sandpaper.**

The last part of any job (apart from clearing up!) is ensuring your work has the appropriate finish. Some jobs, such as joists and supporting frameworks that are not going to be seen, don't need any particular finish, but in other jobs a proper finish is essential. Door and window frames, for instance, need to be prepared to accept paint or varnish. Other items, such as furniture, may require a very fine finish. For most purposes a smoothing plane is used to dress the timber. If a smoother finish is required, sandpaper can be used.

Finish with a plane

A smoothing plane is used to finish a lot of basic woodwork. Always use the plane in the same direction as the grain and make sure the blade is sharp. For curved surfaces you can use a spokeshave – this is a plane with a curved convex or a concave blade.

Using a plane

Finish with sandpaper

Sandpaper has an abrasive material fixed to its surface. It is used to remove arrises (sharp edges on joints) and any other imperfections on surfaces to make them smoother, prior to painting and wood finishing. It can also be used to remove a layer of material (e.g. old paint), or sometimes to make the surface rougher (e.g. as a preparation to gluing).

Sandpaper works a lot like a saw, chisel, or any other cutting tool in your workshop. The particles on sandpaper are made up from a number of sharp edges that cut the wood the same way a saw blade does. The only real difference is that sandpaper, unlike your saw, can't be sharpened, and it abrades surfaces rather than cutting them.

When talking about sandpaper, 'grit' is a reference to the number of abrasive particles per 25 millimetres of sandpaper. The lower the grit number the rougher the sandpaper, and the higher the grit number the smoother the sandpaper. This makes sense if you imagine how small the particles on an 800-grit sandpaper would need to be to fit into a 25 millimetre square of sandpaper. Sandpaper is referred to by the size of its grit (e.g. 150-grit sandpaper) as shown in the table below.

Grit	Common Name	Uses
40–60	Coarse	Heavy sanding and stripping, roughing up the surface.
80–120	Medium	Smoothing of the surface, removing smaller imperfections and marks.
150–180	Fine	Final sanding pass before finishing the wood.
220–240	Very Fine	Sanding between coats of stain or sealer.
280–320	Extra Fine	Removing dust spots or marks between finish coats.
360–600	Super Fine	Fine sanding of the finish to remove some lustre or surface blemishes and scratches.

Figure 7.22 Grades of sandpaper

Developing trowel skills

At the end of this unit you should be able to...

* recognise and select the appropriate hand tools and personal protective equipment required to undertake simple brickwork tasks

* identify different types of construction materials

* identify the bonding arrangement in stretcher bond walling and a range of basic joint finishes

* produce mortar to given specifications

* use hand tools to lay bricks in stretcher bond and form new joint applications

* identify hazards associated with the work and apply safe working practices.

Unit overview

This unit introduces you to the commonly used hand tools, personal protective equipment and craft skills required to construct and maintain basic brickwork structures. Emphasis is placed on the correct selection and safe use of the appropriate tools and equipment used to carry out simple brickwork processes.

There is an opportunity for you to develop an understanding of the principles, methods and safe work practices involved in the preparation and mixing of lime-based mortars for the application of new joint finishes to existing masonry structures.

It is assumed that you have either successfully completed Unit 3: Developing Skills and Working Safely in Construction before starting this unit, or that you will be studying Unit 3 alongside this unit. This unit is internally assessed. To pass it you must complete a practical or written assignment set and marked by your teacher or tutor.

Bricklaying is a fundamental job in the construction industry.

What is a bricklayer?

In this section you will learn about...

✹ the work carried out by bricklayers

✹ skills and qualifications needed to become a qualified bricklayer.

A bricklayer is somebody who competently erects a variety of structures using a wide range of materials. A bricklayer is responsible for making sound structural protection to new and existing buildings.

Bricklayers work with different **masonry** products and **mortar** mixtures to build new walls, garages, houses, factories and offices. They also carry out repair work to existing buildings and premises to keep them in safe condition and habitable. Their role within the construction industry is considered of high importance, and a skilled qualified bricklayer is a priceless asset to any company.

Bricklayers work within a large construction team and perform their work in all weather conditions. To become a qualified bricklayer you need to obtain a minimum of a National Vocational Qualification (NVQ) Level 2 or Level 3 qualification, a Technical Certificate, Key skills in Literacy and Numeracy, pass the health and safety test, gain site experience and possess a good, sound knowledge of the construction industry.

Masonry – this term relates to any solid construction material such as bricks, blocks and stone.

Mortar – mixture of lime, cement, sand and water that is used to fix bricks and other masonry in place.

Hand tools and personal protective equipment

In this section you will learn about...

✹ types of bricklaying tools

✹ good practice with tools and equipment

✹ safe working

✹ personal protective equipment.

A bricklayer needs fewer tools compared to other trades, but they must still be of a good standard and reliable. Good craftsmen take care of their tools and equipment at all times. That way the tools will last a long time, and as you get accustomed to and familiar with particular tools, you will not want to keep replacing them.

Tools can be classified under the following headings:

* Bedding/laying tools

* Levelling tools

* Cutting, measuring and marking tools

* Finishing tools.

Bedding/laying tools

These are tools used for applying, laying and manipulating mortar. They are your main tools and should be carefully looked after. Trowels should be lightly oiled when not in use to prevent them rusting.

Brick/walling trowel

This is a flat diamond-shaped piece of carbon steel with a handle, used for rolling, cutting and applying mortar. The trowel is the most important tool for a bricklayer, and because it gets very heavy use and is prone to damage it must be designed in a robust way. Brick trowels can be bought in different sizes and for left- or right-handed users. Over the years the design of the brick trowel has changed little, the main change being the introduction of foam or rubber handles in contrast to the traditional wooden one.

Pointing trowel

This is a scaled-down size of a brick trowel. It is used to form a weatherstruck and flush joint on brick/block walling. The same care should be taken when purchasing a pointing trowel as a brick trowel. Both tools must be cleaned with a dry cloth when finished with and stored safely.

Brick trowel and pointing trowel

Levelling tools

These are tools that help you ensure that your work is level and **plumb**. They range from very basic tools to sophisticated electronic versions and include:

* spirit level

* lines and pins and corner blocks

* tingle plate

* straight edge

* gauge lath.

Spirit level

DRILL DOWN

Check out some websites of companies that supply building tools. You will get an idea of the range of tools available, and their prices.

Using a straight edge with a spirit level

Spirit level

A spirit level is used to accurately correct the vertical and horizontal alignment of any masonry work. They are made from a metal straight edge with glass tubes inserted into it, which contain a liquid and a bubble of air. The tubes are marked with two lines. When the bubble is positioned exactly dead centre between the two lines, the instrument is completely level (horizontal) or plumb (vertical). There are many different spirit levels on the market; some are adapted for specific tasks, such as a scaffold level, but all are based on the same simple design principle. These days you can also get digital spirit levels that will measure angles for you. A smaller version of a spirit level is called a boat or pocket level.

Lines and pins

These are string lines wrapped around pins which can be pushed firmly into a mortar joint in the walling. They are used to horizontally or vertically align masonry work between two pre-erected corners. The lines ensure accuracy, whilst the pins ensure the lines have a fixed point pinned to the pre-erected corners.

Lines and pins can also be used in conjunction with corner blocks, which secure the lines around the corner of the wall. The advantage of these is that they avoid damage to the mortar joint or brickwork.

Tingle plate

This is used with a string line over a long distance and prevents the line from sagging, which gives a better alignment of the bricks.

Straight edge

Any length of timber or steel that has true parallel sides can be deemed a straight edge. A straight edge is usually used in conjunction with a spirit level to transfer levels across a site. A straight edge should always be reversed end to end after each reading to ensure any inaccuracy is detected.

◈ Gauge lath/storey rod

Brick and block walling must always be to **gauge**. This means that all walling heights must be correctly maintained at all times by the gauge lath, a length of timber marked out with the correct gauges. A gauge lath which is longer than normal and can span more than the height of a standard house is called a storey rod. This is used by a bricklayer to determine at what heights on a building lintels, ceiling joists, window sills etc. are inserted.

> **Gauge** – the correct brick or block height in a wall. Standard brick gauge works to 75 mm high for one course of bricks, 300 mm for four courses.

Measuring and marking tools

The bricklayer will frequently use a selection of these tools to maintain a high degree of craftsmanship. He will use the following tools, usually in conjunction with chalk or pencil:

* steel tape measure
* brick marking gauge
* builder's square
* sliding bevel.

◈ Steel tape measure

This is used to accurately measure items to be cut, such as bricks, blocks, insulation or **damp proof course** (DPC), or simply to measure a piece of work. All brickwork is measured in millimetres and metres, but commonly the tape will have imperial (feet and inches) marked on also. Tapes range in sizes from 2 m to 30 m.

> **Damp proof course (DPC)** – a waterproof layer inserted into a wall to prevent damp from penetrating into the building.

Steel tape measure

◈ Brick marking gauge

This tool is used to determine the length of a brick to be cut. The brick gauge ensures the brick that's cut is maintained to the same size, as the gauge acts as a template.

Builder's square

◈ Builder's square

A builder's square is used for the setting out of 90° angles on houses and extensions. It is usually made from timber or steel and is an invaluable piece of equipment that the bricklayer uses to ensure accuracy of corners to be constructed.

Sliding bevel

◈ Sliding bevel

A sliding bevel is used to maintain angled cuts, which will appear on raking cuts on gable end walling. The bevel is adjusted and tightened using screws that ensure the correct angle required for marking and cutting.

Cutting tools

These are hand tools used to cut or shape solid building materials to size, or for texturing surfaces. Hammers and chisels are the basic cutting tools. There are several types of hammer used for specific jobs. Different chisels are used by the bricklayer with a lump hammer to perform different tasks. All chisels are usually made from toughened steel.

We shall look at:

* club hammer
* brick hammer
* scutch hammer
* bolster chisel
* cold chisel
* plugging chisel.

◈ Club, lump or mash hammer

A club hammer is a steel-headed hammer attached to a shaft or handle. It is a heavy hand tool and is used to hit a chisel when either cutting, chasing or scoring materials.

◈ Brick hammer

This is a lighter hammer than the club hammer and it has a longer head, which has two different ends. One end is square, which can be used to strike a chisel, and the other has a chisel blade, which must be kept sharp. The main purpose of a brick hammer is for rough cutting of bricks and blocks.

Club hammer, brick hammer and scutch hammer

◨ Scutch/comb hammer

This hammer is almost the same shape as a brick hammer but instead of having square and blade ends it has clamps in each end in which different blades can be inserted. Blades can have a chisel edge or a scutch edge, which is like a toothed comb. Blades and scutches can be replaced when they are worn down or have lost the edge on their teeth. The scutch hammer is usually used for trimming, cutting and shaping bricks.

◨ Bolster chisel

A bolster chisel is used to accurately cut bricks and blocks straight. It consists of a blade that is usually 50 mm to 100 mm wide. The edge is toughened for cutting hard materials but the striking end is softer to prevent it shattering and breaking off. Some come with safety grip handles.

◨ Cold chisels

These come in a variety of lengths and widths and are used for different jobs, such as cutting out holes in walls and chasing walls. They are made of forged hardened tempered steel. Some come with safety grip handles.

◨ Plugging chisel

A plugging chisel is tapered to a point and is used to cut out mortar joints from masonry work for repairs. Plugging chisels are made from cast steel and usually only come in one size.

Cold chisels, bolster chisels and plugging chisels must be used with care as sometimes a mushroom head can form on the end, and this can cut the operator's hand. Also, shards of thin metal can fly off a mushroom head when it is struck, and these could go in the operator's eye.

All chisels must be kept sharp to obtain maximum cutting precision.

SAFE✚Y TIP

To avoid injury to hands and eyes, ensure that you grind off mushroom heads that form on your chisels.

Bolster chisel, cold chisel, plugging chisel and chisel with mushroom head

Finishing tools

These tools are used to provide the final appearance to a bricklayer's work.

◪ Jointing iron/bar

This tool is used to put a final touch on mortar joints. It is made from a half round steel bar. When pressed against a mortar joint it will push the mortar into a curved shape making it weather protected. This jointing method can only be achieved when mortar is still soft.

◪ Chariot/joint recesser

A recessing chariot or joint raker is used to rake out soft mortar joints. It has a long metal handle with two wheels and a pin at the end. As you push the raker along a mortar joint the pin scrapes at the mortar and giving a neat recess joint.

◪ Hawk

A hawk, also called a hand board, is used during jointing and re-pointing. It is made of a piece of flat material (plywood, plastic, steel or aluminium) attached to a handle and held horizontally. Mortar can then be placed on the board for ease of use during working.

◪ Hand brush

A soft hand brush is used by the bricklayer after a joint finish has been made. The wall is simply brushed down and any loose mortar on the wall is swept clear from the masonry work.

Jointing iron

Chariot

Hand brush

TRY THIS

Read the following scenarios and determine which pair of tools are most suitable to brickwork activity.

1. You need to cut a hole through a brick wall to fit an extractor fan.

   Tool choice:

   * Brick hammer and hawk

   * Jointing bar and cold chisel

   * Club hammer and plugging chisel

   * Bevel and bolster chisel.

2. You need to re-point cement mortar into cracks in a brick wall.

   Tool choice:

   * Bevel and jointing bar

   * Pointing trowel and hawk

   * Level and brick gauge

   * Pointing trowel and string line.

3. You need to mark out some bricks to be used on a raking cut.

   Tool choice:

   * Level and club hammer

   * Brick gauge and bolster

   * Walling trowel and pins

   * Pencil and bevel.

4. You need to transfer the height of timber pegs across a building site.

   Tool choice:

   * Straight edge and walling trowel

   * Level and straight edge

   * Level and bolster

   * Hawk and builder's square.

5. You need to determine the heights of sills, lintels and frames of a new house.

   Tool choice:

   * Walling trowel and level

   * Tape measure and storey rod

   * Gauge lath and pencil

   * Brick hammer and pins.

Good practice with hand tools

Here are some handy hints for best practice in caring for your tools. Remember, they are your tools, and you are responsible for them.

* Always look after your tools; keep them safe in a tool bag, box or plastic bucket. Tools can be expensive, so store them in a security hut, tool vault, site van or lockable cabin.

* Always use the correct tool for the job. Brick trowels, for instance, are strong and durable enough to cut and trim bricks, but this is not recommended as it could split the blade or chip the brick. This could send flying debris into your eyes.

* Do not let cement mortar build up on trowels or other tools. Always clean tools after use as they can rust if not cleaned and dried properly. Ideally, tools should be cleaned, dried and lightly oiled.

* Hand tools with wooden handles should be kept dry at all times. If they are wet then the handles will eventually rot and crack. Cracks can then turn into splinters, which can injure your hands.

TRY THIS

Think of six other occupations in the construction industry that rely upon a bricklayer to carry out a competent job prior to them undertaking any work.

Write a description of what type of work they do.

Staying safe

It is of mandatory importance that you and other workers stay safe while working with hand tools. You must always consider these guidelines to help you, and others, stay safe.

* Wear the correct clothing for the task.

* Don't wear jewellery.

* Always keep your hands away from sharp points and objects.

* Never misuse any tool.

* Never use the wrong tool for the job.

* Never put any part of your body in front of a cutting edge.

* Never use tools that you have not been given permission to use.

* Make sure tools are in good condition and are cleaned before being returned.

* Keep all work areas clean and tidy.

* Always ask if you are unsure of how to use a tool or piece of equipment.

Personal protective equipment (PPE)

In this section you will learn about...

❋ the correct types of PPE to use as a bricklayer.

SAFE+Y TIP

Before you study this section, read Unit 3: *Developing skills and working safely in construction.*

Types of PPE

Different types of PPE are available, and their quality, size and durability are important when selecting which type to use.

Head protection

Suitable head protection is required on all building sites unless there is absolutely no risk of head injury. Different types of head protection are available, and they all must be to British Standard. The two main types of head protection are:

❋ **hard hats** – heavy duty protection where there is a danger of falling objects

❋ **bump caps** – lighter protection, used where there is a likelihood of bumping the head on low ceilings or projections.

Hard hat

Eye protection

By law eye protection is required if there is any possibility of eye injury. This may be caused by grinding, welding, hammering, using dangerous chemicals, cutting or demolition work. The different types of eye protection that can be used are:

❋ **safety goggles** – made from durable plastic and used to protect the eyes from dust and physical injury

❋ **safety glasses** – also made from durable plastic but not as heavy-duty as goggles and don't fully enclose the eyes. Used to protect the eyes from flying debris

❋ **safety visor** – fire and spark-proof protection for the eyes and face, used with welding equipment and when grinding out mortar as it offers good visibility and rarely mists up.

These provide different methods of protection and durability, but are all very effective. To determine which eye protection to use, a risk assessment should be carried out.

SAFE+Y TIP

All PPE must be thoroughly checked prior to use.

Safety goggles and safety glasses

Ear defenders

Dust mask

Gloves

Safety boots

Ear protection

The different types of ear protection vary due to their purpose but should be comfortable to use and fit for the operation. Common ear protectors are:

* **ear plugs** – single use, made of foam and personal to the user, they fit snugly inside the ear and offer some degree of protection against minor noise

* **ear defenders** – more robust than ear plugs, these cover the ears, sealing them off, and are suitable for a high level of noise. They are not personal to the user and may be used more than once.

Respiratory protection

Bricklayers use a variety of substances and chemicals on site, and they are also exposed to situations which may be dusty. To combat this they must protect their nose and mouth from the inhalation of these noxious substances. Two different types of PPE commonly used are:

* **dust masks** – the most commonly used protection. These are personal to the user, disposable, and help to filter out airborne dust

* **respirators** – used when chemical fumes make it difficult for the operator to breathe without the aid of clean air passing through mouth and nose frequently.

Hand protection

Bricklayers' hands are always prone to abuse every day by the use of abrasive materials, chemical use, tools and equipment and weather elements. Although bricklayers generally dislike laying bricks while wearing gloves, as they like to feel bricks and bed them down properly, they should protect their hands wherever possible when transporting bricks and other building materials. It is also important to try and keep your hands dry and regularly washed to prevent dermatitis. There are several levels of hand protection:

* **barrier cream** – the basic level of protection for skin and hands. Barrier cream is rubbed on to the skin and helps protect the skin against water and against drying out.

* **gloves** – these must have a good fit and are used solely for their purpose. They protect the hands from some chemicals, minor cuts and abrasions when dealing with building materials.

* **gauntlets** – heavy-duty gloves, which can be used to give added wrist protection when carrying objects such as glass.

Foot protection

Feet are the most obvious part of the body that can be injured or damaged on site. All footwear used on site should have non-slip treads, steel toecaps and possibly a toughened sole to withstand a puncture from a nail. Two types of foot protection are commonly worn by bricklayers:

* **safety boots** – these have steel toecaps to protect against any materials dropped on the feet. Safety boots must fit the operative correctly and allow the feet to breathe.

* **Wellington boots** – used when concreting, digging or working in trenches. These should also be fitted with steel toecaps.

◐ Body protection

Bricklayers work in a variety of different conditions, and body protection usually includes:

* **overalls** – made from tough cotton or cotton/synthetic mix fabric, these protect against chemical splashes to the skin and also protect the clothing from dust and debris.

* **high-visibility vests** – these are mandatory for bricklayers to wear on site to alert other workers using machinery or other mechanical equipment to their presence.

◐ Height restraints

From time to time bricklayers may have to work at height. In such situations it is mandatory to be fitted with a suitable safety harness. These are straps fitted across the body and usually attached by a belt to an anchor point on the working platform.

High-visibility vest

Safety harness

SAFE✝Y TIP

Bricklayers on site should ensure they have high factor sun cream protection, particularly in the summer months, to protect skin against ultra violet rays, which can cause skin cancer.

TRY THIS

Read the scenarios below and select the appropriate level of PPE you think is required to suitably complete the task. As a guide we have given you how many items of PPE are required.

1. Re-point a chimney stack on a three-storey building from a suitable working platform. Five items of PPE.

2. You need to concrete the foundations for a new garage on site. Five items of PPE.

3. You need to erect a half-brick wall at the side of a house which is currently undergoing some alteration work. Three items of PPE.

4. A block wall needs demolishing inside an old farmhouse. Six items of PPE.

5. Clean mortar stains from a newly erected wall. Six items of PPE.

6. You need to cut a hole through a concrete wall using a pneumatic breaker. Seven items of PPE.

7. You have been asked to unload some steel lintels from the delivery truck. Three items of PPE.

8. An old manhole needs unblocking before it is re-pointed. Five items of PPE.

Solid brick walling – half-brick walling

In this section you will learn about...

* **basic setting out**

* **bricks**

* **brick and block bonding**

* **erecting solid walling.**

Half-brick walling – The simplest form of brick walling. The wall is the thickness of half a brick.

The aim of this section is to help you understand the basic principles to apply when erecting brick and block walling to straight lengths in a stretcher bond wall with stopped ends. It will look at finishings and different components used for bricklaying.

Setting out

Setting out of any structure requires a great deal of patience and concentration. This is the measuring out and positioning of the brick structure.

The nature of the job will determine the degree of the accuracy that is required and the final outcome of the work.

A good selection of tools and equipment is needed to professionally set out any structure. The main tools required are:

* tape measure

* builder's square

* straight edge

* builder's lines.

Good bricklayers who are expert at setting out structures are relied upon by their employers to set out work on the site – thus saving the expense of hiring a civil engineer.

A bricklayer must be able to read a tape measure and apply basic mathematical calculations to set out the work to be done. Once competent at setting out basic squares and rectangles, you will then have to learn how to set out irregular shapes, for instance for conservatory bases.

Bricklayers not only determine the positions of houses, walls, doors and windows, but they also establish depths for foundations to be excavated and quantities of material to be ordered, and they can also be responsible for the positioning of all drainage components in and around the site.

case study

Ron, a highly qualified and skilled bricklayer, owns a bricklaying company and employs four other skilled workers and three labourers. His company has been established for four years and had been slowly growing, but business has fallen off a bit recently. In fact the company's workers often turn up late for jobs, materials are frequently delivered late, and the company is always taking on more work than it can comfortably fulfil. Ron misses important calls from clients as he often forgets to charge up his mobile. Ron has also received some customer complaints that his workers are not competent, so he finds he is constantly running around after his employees putting things right and trying to placate angry customers. Sadly, Ron's once-excellent reputation is slowly disappearing.

Questions and activities

1. Why do you think the company is doing so badly?

2. What could you advise Ron to do to put things right in the short term?

3. Is there any other sort of worker Ron could employ to help his business other than labourers and tradespeople?

4. Are there any long-term changes Ron should make?

5. Think about best practice in running a construction business. What would be your top ten best practices?

Bricks

The vast majority of bricks used in construction are made from clay, concrete or calcium silicate (sand/lime). The clay is extruded or moulded, then fired in a kiln. The standard size of a brick is 215 mm long x 102.5 mm wide x 65 mm high. Bricks are made in a uniform shape and can be easily bonded (laid) in a number of ways so a variety of patterns can be achieved. They are designed to have a variety of strengths depending on their purpose. There are three basic types:

* **common brick** – has no particular finish, or face, so is generally used to construct inside walls or other walls where appearance is not important.

* **facing brick** – designed for its decorative appearance with a finished surface. It is used on houses, walls and the outer **leaf** of most buildings.

* **engineering brick** – dense brick used where heavy loads are imposed, for instance retaining walls, or where water barriers are required, for instance damp proof courses and inspection chambers.

Facing, common and engineering bricks

Different cut bricks

A bricklayer must occasionally use cut bricks to erect an appropriate wall to building standards. Cut bricks most commonly used are:

* **bats** – bricks cut along the face that leave the header intact

* **closers** – bricks that are cut along the header of a brick that leave the stretcher face of the brick intact, e.g. queen closer, king closer, mitred closer.

These bricks can usually be cut using a hammer and bolster but may require cutting with a masonry saw.

Bat and closer

Blocks

Blocks are six times bigger on the face than bricks. They are usually 440 mm long x 215 mm high x 75 mm, 100 mm, 150 mm or 225 mm thick. Blocks are mainly used for internal walls or for external walls that are to be rendered or clad. Blocks are generally made from concrete or lightweight aggregates.

* **concrete blocks** – are dense and often very heavy

* **lightweight blocks** – often have air bubbles put into them to aid their insulation qualities.

The main advantage of blocks over bricks is the increased speed of laying them per metre than bricks because they are larger, and their thermal insulation values. Bricks and blocks have sharp corners and coarse textures, so gloves must be worn when handling and storing them.

Lightweight block

Brick and block bonding

Brickwork and blockwork is laid in a variety of ways to achieve strength and decoration in the walling. Bricks and blocks must be placed correctly on top of each other so that any loads placed upon the wall are passed down through the wall. This is called **bonding**, and bricks and blocks must be bonded appropriately to avoid any structural problems. The basic bond that a bricklayer uses is called **stretcher** bond.

Stretcher bond

This is the main bond used in general house building. Stretcher bond can be built in either single, double or cavity wall construction. Stretcher bond is built showing the long face of the brick. Bricks are laid in **courses**, **header** to header, and the **joints** squeezed to 10 mm.

Erection of walling

Bricklayers become neater and quicker at their craft with age and experience, but patience and good planning are always essential when learning and applying their trade. Before they master the art of laying bricks, bricklayers must be competent at loading up their materials and preparing their area before they commence bricklaying.

Dry bonding

Once ready to lay bricks, the bricklayer will **dry bond** the wall out. This is the laying of bricks with a gap of 10 mm in between them, called a perpendicular, or '**perp**', all the way along the proposed first course of a wall. This determines whether the wall will work accurately with full bricks or whether and where any cut bricks should be positioned. Cut bricks are usually placed in the centre of walls or under windows or doors to avoid them being unsightly. Dry bonding is done prior to erection of any brickwork.

Constructing the wall

The correct method to erect any wall is to start at the ends of the wall and erect the **quoins**, or corners, first.

This is the slowest part of a bricklayer's job, and time must be taken to ensure the wall is correctly erected plumb, gauge aligned, ranged and true in all senses.

Once the corners have been erected either side of the proposed wall they are generally jointed up before the mortar gets too stiff. The procedure that follows is termed **walling to a line** and is regarded as the easiest and quickest method.

The bricklayer attaches a builder's line to corner blocks or pins, connects them to the pre-erected corners and pulls the line taut. If the length of proposed wall is of a great distance then, the line should be tingled to prevent sagging of the line. Once the line is set up the bricklayer lays the mortar bed and proceeds to bed bricks down to the height of the line.

Types of stretcher bonding

* **Reverse bond**

  This is used on a wall where the pattern bond at either end of a wall cannot be the same. If a stretcher bond wall has a stretcher at one end it will have a stretcher at the other end of the wall. Vice versa for a course that starts with a header at one end and finishes with a header on the same course. Reverse bond starts with a stretcher and ends with a header or starts with a header and ends with a stretcher. This bond avoids putting cuts in the middle of the wall.

> **Stretcher** – the long side of a brick.
>
> **Header** – the end of a brick.
>
> **Joint** – the gap between laid bricks, filled with mortar.
>
> **Course** – a single row of brickwork.
>
> **Perp** – a perpendicular joint in brickwork.

Wall with pre-erected corner ready to line in

* **Broken bond**

    Broken bond is used when a wall has been set out and its bond doesn't work accurately for full bricks, so cut bricks are needed. It is usual to position the cut bricks under doors or windows. Cut bricks in the wall must not be less than a half bat, otherwise they will not conform to building regulations.

Calculation formulas for brickwork

The area of brickwork is measured in **square metres** (m^2). Bricklayers work to a ratio of 60 bricks per metre square in a half-brick thick wall. If a bricklayer is working in a walling thickness in excess of half-brick thick then other formulas must be applied, depending on the bond to be used. For stretcher bond walling, 60 bricks/per m^2 half-brick and 120 bricks/per m^2 for one brick thick walling is used.

Bricklayers must possess good skills in calculation for two main reasons:

* they need to give people a price to undertake work

* they need to give a calculated estimate for materials required for a job.

One metre square – this is 1 metre in length times 1 metre in height.

To calculate accurately the number of bricks and blocks needed for a job, a bricklayer uses his tape measure to measure the proposed walling, or reads and interprets information given from drawings.

Bricklayers need to take into account window and door openings, which need to be deducted, and also the possibility of work to be built underground. Once all areas have been determined, the area given should be multiplied by 60 bricks if it is to be built in half-brick thick walling (as there are 60 bricks per square metre) or 120 bricks if the proposed wall is to be built 1 brick thick (as there are 120 blocks per square metre).

> e.g. 45 square metres of brickwork to be erected
>
> 45 x 60 = **2700 bricks required**

If walling is to be built in blockwork then the area in metres is multiplied by 10 (as there are 10 blocks per square metre).

> e.g. 45 square metres of blockwork to be erected
>
> 45 x 10 = **450 blocks required**

TRY THIS

1. A half-brick wall is to be built in stretcher bond 9 metres long and 2 metres high. Calculate how many bricks are required.

2. A one-brick thick wall is to be erected in stretcher bond 12 metres long and 1.5 metres high. Calculate how many bricks are required.

3. How many blocks are required to erect a wall 17 metres long and 3 metres high?

4. Work out how many bricks and blocks are required to build the side of a cavity wall that has a surface area of 15 metres square.

5. Determine the number of blocks required to erect a cavity wall that is 10 metres long and 2 metres high. The wall also has an opening, which must be deducted, and this has an area of 1.5 metres square.

New joint finishes

In this section you will learn about...

✳ **mortar preparation**

✳ **determining mortar quantities**

✳ **joint application.**

Mortar preparation

Mortar is the name given to a material that bonds masonry together. It is used for bedding and jointing the various components together and it is made from:

✳ sand

✳ cement

✳ plasticiser

✳ water

✳ colouring agents.

Mixed mortar

The mortar needs to be 'workable', which means it should be soft, smooth and easy to roll and spread on a wall. The correct mix proportion for mortar in building construction is one of the most important factors in providing strength, colour and finish. All components – yellow sand, cement, plasticiser – play significant but different parts in establishing a good mix.

Well graded – sand that has small, medium and large particles in it.

Mortar should not be stronger than the brick or block. If this is the case, then bricks or blocks would crack during settlement instead of mortar joints cracking. If the mortar is too strong, more sand should be added to the mix to reduce the cement strength in the mix.

◻ Mortar components

✳ **Sand**
Sand for brick and blocklaying should be soft, clean and **well graded**. A sand that has even-sized particles is deemed poorly graded.

✳ **Cement**
Cement is the binding agent in mortar. It is used to combine sand and water particles with a chemical reaction that sets the mortar into a hard layer that holds the bricks and blocks together.

✳ **Plasticiser**
A plasticiser plays an important part in mixing mortar as it makes the mortar 'workable'. Plasticiser was traditionally lime powder mixed into the mortar, but nowadays it is often replaced by a liquid additive that is added to the mix.

Plasticiser, cement and sand

✳ **Water**
Water used in mortar mixing must be potable – that is, clean enough to drink. Dirty water will contaminate the mix and may adversely affect how it works, looks and sets.

* **Colouring agents**

   Occasionally mortar colours may need to be changed for the sake of appearance. This is usually done by adding a powder or liquid pigment to the mortar. If a large mix is required it is usually best to order a coloured sand, which may be a cheaper alternative than adding a colouring agent to every mix. It also means that you will keep the colour consistent throughout the job.

Cement mixer

Mortar mix ratios

Mortar mixes change from job to job; therefore this must be confirmed with the architect or manager prior to the commencement of any task. Mortars are mixed in a ratio proportion for each specific job e.g. 1:1:5, this means 1:cement; 1:lime; 5:sand. This ensures materials are accurately 'gauged' and an equal colour, strength and durability is determined. The best way of gauging materials is by using buckets or containers sometimes known as gauge boxes. This ensures each material is identical every time.

Mixing mortar

Mortar can be mixed by either hand or mixer. Hand mixing with a shovel can be tedious and difficult to maintain consistency. Machine mixing is quicker and produces a consistent, quality mix.

EVIDENCE

Find out the mortar mix proportions for the following types of masonry work:

* Block partition walls
* Work below the ground
* Facing brickwork on a street house
* An inspection chamber
* Re-pointing of a chimney stack.

Jointing

Joint application

Jointing and pointing refer to two different methods of finishing mortar joints between masonry. All mortar joints when completed should be allowed to dry then lightly brushed with a soft-bristled brush. This removes excess mortar that might stick to the joint or is loosely hanging on the brickwork.

Jointing

This term is used to describe the operation of finishing mortar joints as work proceeds. The joint finish is applied using the same mortar that has been used to bed and bond the materials together. Jointing is carried out using a jointing tool shaped in a semicircular channel and smoothed across the mortar joints.

When you do the jointing depends on the absorbency rate of the material being used, for example engineering bricks will need more time to set.

Jointing is usually preferred to pointing because:

* it has an increased structural strength

* it means a considerable reduction in labour costs

* it is less likely to be damaged by rain or frost

* it has a consistent colour of the mortar joint.

Pointing

The term pointing refers to the mortar joints being finished after the structure is completed, or when a structure needs to be re-pointed due to considerable decay of the mortar joints.

Before re-pointing, the face of the brickwork must be assessed and the condition of the wall noted in order to determine whether to re-point or demolish the job. It is essential that all joints are raked out to a depth of no less than 12 mm and not exceeding 19 mm. When re-pointing, old mortar must be fully removed to the required depth to enable the fresh mortar to bond to the masonry.

Re-pointing

In order to help the existing mortar and brickwork to bond to the new mortar you should dampen the face of the wall or add a bonding agent to the mortar mix. Brick joints can be sprayed using a controlled gun, which ensures the joints are adequately dampened and also prevents over-soaking, which can result in the shrinkage of newly formed joints. The spray also removes any dust particles that will have formed on the brickwork and which would prevent new mortar bonding to it.

External weatherstruck joint

This finish is the best type of joint to resist weather penetration in exposed areas, as the slope of the finished joints allows rain to run off the surface rather than lie in the joint. The finish is applied using a pointing trowel or brick trowel. It is good for covering any irregularities and creates a straight edge. The surface of the joint is slightly pressed back to the left side of perpendicular joints and along the top of bed (horizontal) joints and thus compacted by the pressure of the trowel blade. This joint is very suitable for engineering bricks. All perpendicular joints should be completed before the bed joints so that a continuous joint is kept along the bed.

Creating a weatherstruck joint

Flush or rubbed joint (bagged off)

These joints are achieved by leaving the mortar joint full or flush from the trowel blade when laying the bricks, so that the mortar is flush with the face of the bricks. Any holes are filled in with a rubber or sacking pad (traditionally a scrunched-up cement bag), and the surface finished off by using the pad or a wood or plastic block to compact the surface. This joint should not be used on exposed areas. This brick joint is most suitable for handmade bricks as it enhances the old-world, rustic appearance. This finish can only be done at the same time as construction.

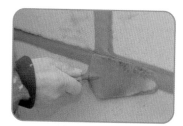

Creating a flush joint

Key/half round/bucket handle/ironed/ tooled joint

All these terms describe the most popular and modern type of joint finish. This joint is achieved by using a purpose-made semi-circular jointing tool or a

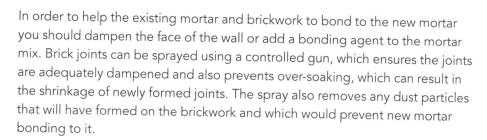

12 mm – 19 mm diameter steel rod bent to the required shape. Both jointing tools provide a concave finish when pressed on to the mortar joints to compact the finish. This joint is used internally and externally, and is probably the quickest, most favoured method of decoratively finishing mortar joints. This joint is suitable for most types of brick- and blockwork and is carried out as work progresses.

◘ Recessed joint

This type of joint finish is best used with bricks or blocks that have only minimal variation in their sizes. A recessed joint is not suitable for load-bearing walls or walls that appear to be in danger from severe weather elements. It is made with a purpose-made tool called a chariot which, when pushed along the wall, scrapes the mortar from the front of the joint. The recess that is formed must not exceed 19 mm in depth. This type of jointing is carried out as the work progresses. A suitable brick for this joint would be one with sharp arrises, for instance engineering brick.

A recessed joint

WHAT WOULD YOU DO?

You have been asked to construct a small garden wall for a client. The site has a northern aspect and is quite exposed to the weather. What type of bricks would you recommend, and what type of jointing would be suitable?

TRY THIS

You will now be assessed at your competency to erect a 2-brick square detached pier 12 courses high. The four different sides of the pier will be finished with a weatherstruck joint, a recessed joint, a half round joint and a flush joint.

The marking scheme that your assessor will use will take into consideration the following:

* identification of correct tools and equipment
* plumbing
* gauging
* levelling
* quality of joint finish
* health and safety considerations
* alignment of brickwork
* time taken
* cleanliness of your workstation.

The task is to be internally assessed by your assessor, and you are encouraged to self-assess the model with your assessor.

Health, safety and welfare

In this section you will learn about...

* **how to minimize workplace hazards**

* **how to maintain a clean and tidy workspace.**

How to minimize workplace hazards

All work undertaken on site usually has been risk-assessed prior to anyone starting any work. A risk assessment is a careful examination of the hazards and risks that are apparent on building sites and control measures that are put in place to protect people from harm. You will find more on risk assessment in Unit 3.

The main hazards particularly associated with bricklaying are:

* lifting heavy loads (manual handling)

* use of hazardous substances, particularly mortar

* height hazards

* risks from falling objects.

Manual handling

Bricklaying involves a lot of lifting and carrying, from bags of cement to hods of bricks. You must ensure that you know how to lift heavy materials safely. Refer to Unit 3 in this book for more on safe manual handling. Where possible, use gloves to protect your hands when dealing with bricks, blocks and other hard, sharp-edged or heavy materials.

Use of hazardous substances

One of the main substances you will have to use as a bricklayer is mortar. You must therefore be aware of the hazards associated with this substance, and your duty to safely mix, prepare and use it. The materials used in mortar mixing and application are particularly dangerous to health. The main problem is that unmixed mortar includes powder that can damage the skin, eyes and lungs if the irritant ingredients of cement and lime are not used correctly. To prevent mortar damaging the skin and lungs, PPE must be worn at all time when handling the powdered materials. Depending on the circumstances, this will include barrier cream, gloves, dust mask and boots.

Inhalation of cement or lime dust can cause breathing difficulties and make pre-existing conditions, such as asthma, worse. If you experience any health problems as a result of dealing with mortar, you must seek medical advice and take all the safety steps necessary to reduce future risk. Avoid skin contact with

SAFE+Y TIP

The construction industry has over 13,000 reported accidents every year; many of these are fatalities. To make sure you are not one of them, always use the correct PPE and follow all safety instructions to the letter.

SAFE+Y TIP

If you are unsure how to lift something, or think something is too heavy for you to lift on your own, always seek assistance. A hurt back is more damaging to your career as a bricklayer than hurt pride.

SAFE+Y TIP

You should ensure that cement, lime and plasticisers are stored safely when not in use. Opened bags and containers should be properly closed or resealed.

mixed mortar where possible. Use barrier cream and/or gloves, and wash and moisturise your hands after dealing with mortar to reduce the risk of dermatitis.

Height hazards

As a bricklayer there will be times when you will have to work at height from access equipment such as ladders, platforms and scaffolding. Before you work on access equipment, your supervisor must ensure that the equipment is of the appropriate type and gives you adequate safe access to work. You must also be able to safely get on to and off the equipment. Your supervisor should also ensure that the equipment has been safely erected. It is your responsibility not to tamper with the equipment and to report any problems with it that you notice.

Here are some basic tips to follow when working at height:

* Check access equipment is secure and risk-assessed before using it.
* Do not use damaged equipment.
* Be wary about working at height in windy weather.
* Do not tamper with access equipment.
* Report any damage or other concerns you may have about the equipment.
* Wear the appropriate PPE, including a harness, if required.
* Do not fool around on access equipment.

If you have a genuine fear of heights, you must think very carefully about whether you are fitted to a career as a bricklayer. It is very unlikely that you will be able to avoid working at height in this line of work, and you could put your safety, and that of others, at risk if you ignore this.

Falling objects

On any building site there is always the risk of objects falling from height. A colleague might accidentally drop a brick or a tool when working on a scaffold; high wind can dislodge unfixed objects, and so on. To protect yourself it is essential that you always wear a hard hat when working in areas where there is a risk of falling objects. That includes almost everywhere on a construction site.

Maintenance of a tidy workplace

Keeping your work area tidy is vital. If you leave tools or bricks lying around when you are not using them, for instance, this will present a trip hazard. Always follow these simple rules.

* Put tools away when you are not using them.
* Ensure you do not leave discarded bricks, blocks, ties or other materials lying around.
* Clean up all unused mortar when you are finished.
* Close all bags and containers (for instance cement bags and plasticiser containers) when not in use.
* Clean up spilt water or other liquids where they might present a slip hazard.

SAFE+Y TIP

If a ladder is damaged in any way, it must be disposed of and not repaired, as the safety of any repair cannot be guaranteed.

EVIDENCE

When you are next on site, ask your supervisor if you can carry out a risk assessment of any access equipment that is being used. Write up the assessment, including any recommendations, and show your supervisor.

Developing painting and decorating skills

At the end of this unit you should be able to...

* recognise and select appropriate hand tools, materials and personal protective equipment (PPE) to carry out simple painting and decorating tasks

* use hand tools and equipment to apply either water-based or solvent-based paints to new or previously painted surfaces

* use hand tools and equipment to apply either preparatory or non-patterned wallpapers to walls

* apply safe working practices

* clean the work area, tools and equipment adequately and return all equipment safely back to storage.

9

Unit overview

This unit introduces you to the commonly used hand tools, equipment and craft skills required to perform basic painting and decorating operations. Such operations will include the application of paint to either new or previously painted surfaces and the application of either preparatory or non-patterned wallpapers to walls.

It is assumed that you will either have successfully completed Unit 3: *Developing skills and working safely in construction* before starting this unit, or that you will be studying Unit 3 alongside this unit. This unit is internally assessed. To pass it you must complete a practical or written assignment set and marked by your teacher or tutor.

A professional painter and decorator at work.

What is a painter and decorator?

In this section you will learn about...

* **the work carried out by painters and decorators**

* **the skills and qualifications needed to become a qualified painter and decorator.**

The main reasons why we paint and decorate are:

* protection – to protect the surface of walls, fixtures etc.

* identification – to provide visual information such as shop names, signs etc.

* decoration – to make a surface, room or area look good

* sanitation – to make a surface easy to clean.

Painters and decorators work inside and outside of buildings. They sometimes work at ground level but most of the time they work at height, usually on access equipment to reach the area to be painted or decorated.

Work carried out by painters and decorators

There are two main project types that painters and decorators will work on. These are:

* new build

* repainting and redecorating.

New build – a newly constructed building.

New build

A new build will need painting before it is sold. The painter will paint the ceiling, walls and any woodwork inside the house, and any woodwork, garage doors, railings and gates to the outside of the house. To work on new build properties you are likely to either be employed by a large company that specialises in new construction, or by a contractor who is hired by a larger construction company to do the work.

Repainting and redecorating

Residence – property where someone lives. This can include houses, bungalows, flats etc.

Painters and decorators are also employed by property owners to repaint or redecorate a **residence**, office or factory. This can involve the removal of wallpaper, preparation of surfaces, painting of the woodwork and reapplication of wallpaper. People employed in this type of painting and decorating are often sole traders or people working for small companies. Remember, no matter what the job or the company you work for, all jobs include clearing up of the work area on completion, and maintenance and responsibility for storage of working tools and materials.

Skills and qualifications

Painters and decorators must work to high skills level to produce quality workmanship. They may be required to produce specialist decorative effects and finishes, for instance imitation of marble and certain timbers, rag rolling, sponging, gliding, stencilling and signwriting. To be able to do this, all painters and decorators must be qualified to the necessary level. All newly qualified tradespeople will have followed and achieved an apprenticeship framework of qualifications which include a National/Scottish Vocational Qualification (N/SVQ) at Level 2 or Level 3, a Technical Certificate, Key Skills in Literacy and Numeracy and a health and safety test. To achieve Level 3 will usually take three years.

TRY THIS

You want to become a painter and decorator when you leave school. List as many jobs as you can that you think a painter and decorator would carry out. Who would you talk to about finding out more about becoming a painter and decorator?

Staying safe as a painter and decorator

In this section you will learn about...

❋ **how to stay safe as a painter and decorator**

❋ **parts of the body you must protect.**

SAFE╋Y TIP

Before you study this section, make sure you have looked at Unit 3: *Developing skills and working safely in construction.*

How to stay safe as a painter and decorator

All painters and decorators work with materials that could be dangerous to health and safety. They also work above ground level, using stepladders, ladders, scaffolding and other items to gain access to areas at height. You need to be aware of these risk factors and work safely. Safety is everyone's concern. You are not only responsible for your own safety, but for that of others around you. Remember, your negligence or fooling around could lead to someone else getting hurt, so work responsibly at all times.

In order to work safely you need to know about:

❋ personal protective equipment (PPE)

❋ working at height

❋ harmful agents.

A painter and decorator wearing PPE

Personal Protective Equipment (PPE)

PPE should be issued by your employer, school, college or training centre, and must be worn by you when required. During workshop activities you must always wear overalls and steel toecapped boots.

Other PPE you may be required to wear are:

* head protection

* gloves – e.g. gauntlets or chemical resistant gloves

* eye protection – e.g. goggles or visors

* ear defenders

* safety boots

* bib and brace overalls or boiler suits

* breathing equipment e.g. respirators or dust masks.

You will be advised by your teacher, trainer or supervisor what PPE to wear for each task.

Working at height

When you carry out a painting and decorating task you may have to work at height. If you are under 18 years of age you are not allowed to work over two metres above ground level. The new regulations state that safety when working at heights is 'from the ground up'. Research has found that :

* 4,000 people are injured every year falling from height

* 50 per cent of fatal accidents in construction are caused by falls from height

* over 50 per cent of major injuries result from falls from below two metres

* falls from height cost £400 million per year.

Note that most major injuries result from falls below two metres, so you must be safety conscious even when working from relatively low heights. When you are carrying out a practical task, your teacher or supervisor will advise you what equipment to use when working above ground level.

Harmful agents

Many of the substances you work with as a painter and decorator can be harmful if **ingested** or may cause sensitive or allergic reactions if touched. Paints, thinners and adhesives should all be treated with caution. In addition to modern materials, old paint coatings can be hazardous. Some contain **toxic** or other harmful materials such as lead. Old paint coatings will also have absorbed dirt and bacteria during their life. Some wallpaper pastes contain anti-fungal materials which can be toxic.

Ingestion – if harmful substances in the materials you work with get into the stomach they can cause considerable discomfort such as diarrhoea, sickness and symptoms of food poisoning. The use of PPE, such as respirators and dust masks, helps to prevent such problems. In addition, you should always wash your hands thoroughly at the end of a job and particularly before eating.

Ingest – take a substance into the stomach, usually via the mouth, for instance by eating.

Toxic – poisonous.

To avoid ingesting harmful substances you should:

* always eat away from the work area and wash your hands before eating

* always remove overalls before eating

* not bite your fingernails.

🗣 Skin

Lack of proper care of the skin can result in dermatitis, which affects people in different ways and with varying severity. In a mild form it may result in slight irritation or redness of the skin; in more severe dermatitis the skin may harden, blister or crack, becoming exposed to a variety of infections. Severe cases can take years to heal. See Unit 3 page 59.

To prevent dermatitis you should wear suitable gloves. Use barrier cream if exposure is to be of short duration, and use only soap and water or skin cleaners when washing your hands. Remember, if you are not sure, ask your teacher or supervisor, or check the information from the supplier of the material.

SAFE✚Y TIP

Never use white spirit or any solvent to remove paint from the skin. White spirit is an irritant and can cause dry skin and dermatitis.

Hand tools, equipment and personal protective equipment

In this section you will learn about...

* **the different types of tools and equipment used by a painter and decorator and how to use them safely**

* **the different types of materials used by a painter and decorator**

* **the correct PPE to use when using materials and hand tools.**

SAFE✚Y TIP

Stay safe when using hand tools. See the list of general guidelines in Unit 3.

Hand tools (excluding paintbrushes and wallpapering tools)

In any job in construction you require tools and equipment. Hand tools are the basic tools used to carry out a job. They are not powered by electricity or compressed air, they are powered by your bodily force.

Paint scraper

🗣 Paint scraper

This is also called a broad knife. Various sizes are available in blade widths of 25/50/75/100 mm. A good-quality knife has a hardwood handle riveted to a tempered steel blade. Most have a stiff blade suitable for scraping loose paint and wallpaper. When not in use, ensure the blade is clean and protected by a suitable cover.

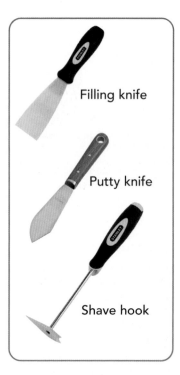

Filling knife

Putty knife

Shave hook

🖸 Filling knife

This is similar to a paint scraper but the blade is thinner and more flexible to allow working of filler into cracks in a surfaces. You should always use a **hand board** to carry filler.

🖸 Putty knife

Also called a stopper or glazing knife, this is used to apply facing and bedding **putty** to wood and metal windows when glazing or replacing broken or cracked panes of glass. A putty knife is also used for filling nail holes and cracks in woodwork. The edge is used to bevel the surface of the putty to give a neat finish. When not in use, the blade should be cleaned. Always check the blade before use for damage or dirt as these will leave marks on the finished putty surface.

🖸 Shave hook

This has a metal head at right angles to the handle shaft. The head has a bevelled cutting edge round the edge and is available in three shapes:

* triangular
* pear-shaped
* a combination of the two.

It is used to scrape paint debris from mouldings and to cut out cracks in plaster surfaces before filling.

🖸 Paint kettle

Also called a paint can or work pot, a paint kettle is made of galvanised sheet iron, black sheet steel, zinc, aluminium alloy or plastic. It is used to hold a convenient quantity of paint decanted (poured) from the manufacturer's container. You could also use empty dry manufacturers' containers as paint kettles.

🖸 Paint roller trays

Paint roller trays are used to hold paint for roller application. They are designed to ensure an even take-up of paint. They commonly come in two forms:

* a rectangular metal or plastic tray; various sizes to take rollers from 150 to 350 mm wide
* a tank bucket or scuttle with either a raised side or a wire grid. Several sizes are available containing up to 10 litres of paint.

Hand board or **hawk** – a board with a handle underneath that allows it to be carried flat, on which you can carry mixed filler, putty and suchlike.

Putty – an oil-based filler that sets very hard. Used for fixing glass into windows, facing surfaces, filling holes and fixing other items in place.

Paint kettle and paint roller tray

Paint rollers

Rollers are used to apply coatings to various surfaces and allow paints to be applied to surfaces quickly, evenly and economically. Most rollers consist of a frame in which a sleeve is inserted. The sleeve is covered with various materials:

* foam or sponge sleeves to apply gloss coating

* lambswool sleeves in short, medium or long **pile** are used to apply most paints to flat and textured surfaces

* **synthetic** fibre sleeves are a cheaper alternative to the lambswool and are harder wearing

* mohair sleeves are used to apply oil-based paints. They are available in short and medium pile.

There are two main types of roller frame:

* single arm rollers

* double arm rollers.

Double arm rollers can hold longer roller sleeves up to 300 mm.

Paint roller

Pile – fibres cut and fixed to a surface.

Synthetic – something man-made, manufactured rather than produced naturally.

TRY THIS

Collect all the tools listed so far in this unit, lay them out and take a photograph. Place the print into your portfolio with a description of the task (date and sign the back of the print).

Paint brushes

The most common way to apply paint to surfaces is to use a paint brush. There are many types of paint brush that can be purchased from suppliers to carry out the application of numerous types of paints, varnishes and stains.

Selecting brushes:

Do not purchase cheap brushes as they will not stand up to the rigours of daily use over long periods of time. When you are buying your brushes you should consider:

* What are you going to paint?

* What type of paint are you applying?

* Is the brush comfortable to hold?

* Is the brush well made?

The quality of paint brushes can make the difference between the finished result meeting the standards required by industry or standards accepted by the do-it-yourself (DIY) sector.

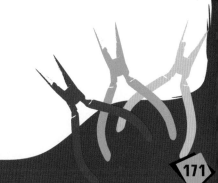

Filling

Stock

Handle

A paint brush

◪ Parts of the brush

There are four main parts to a brush.

* **Handle** – usually made of hardwood such as beech, ash or elm but could also be made of plastic.

* **Stock** – the means by which the handles are fixed to the fillings: usually made from nickel-plated polished steel. There are two types:

  – sheet metal riveted to the handle

  – seamless type pressed on to the handle.

* **Setting** – an adhesive which cements the filaments together at the root. Main types used are vulcanised rubber or a synthetic resin, usually epoxy.

* **Filling** – the fibres of the brush.

There are four main types of brush filling.

* **Pure bristle** – this term applies only to hairs from the pig, boar or hog. As domesticated pigs have only a small amount of short, soft hair, the bristles used in paint brushes come from wild pigs, boars or hogs found mainly in Vietnam, China and India.

Chinese bristles are of high quality, very resilient and black in colour. Indian bristles are rather coarse, longer in length than Chinese bristle, and vary in colour. Vietnam bristles are of good quality. The main properties of bristle are:

– strength and resilience: they can have a long **length out** yet still work well and hold the weight of paint

– serrations or scales like minute teeth along the length of the bristle. These prevent the hairs lying too close togethe,r allowing the brush to hold more paint

– split tip or **flag** which provides a fine tip for **laying off**

– a natural taper from root to tip

– a natural lean or curl.

* **Horsehair** – obtained from the tails and manes of horses. This hair has little spring and no taper. It is sometimes mixed with pure bristle to produce a softer and cheaper brush.

* **Man-made fibre** (synthetic) – these can be nylon, Tynex, Perlon or Orel. These types of filling can be made to imitate bristle. They can be tapered and flagged. They do not give serrations and they do not hold the paint as well as pure bristle. They are very springy, and recovery is equal to, if not better than, pure bristle. They are more hard-wearing and not affected by chemicals. These types of brushes have become very popular in recent years.

* **Natural fibre** – obtained from grass and plants, sourced mainly from Mexico. They have no taper and no serrations but can be flagged mechanically. They are coarse with very poor resilience and usually mixed with pure bristle or horsehair to reduce cost.

Length out – the amount of visible filling.

Laying off – the last stroke of the brush over the wet paint film, usually vertical to the surface.

EVIDENCE

Sketch and make a notes about the following brush fillings. This will help you decide whether to purchase a cheap or an expensive brush for a particular job.

1. Pure bristle

2. Horsehair

3. Nylon

4. Fibre

Ask your teacher, tutor or supervisor to check your answers and insert them into your portfolio.

Types of brushes

* **Flat paint** or **varnish brush** – usually pure bristle but also available in man-made filaments.

  – Use: to apply most types of paint to most surfaces.

  – Size: 25 mm, 37 mm, 50 mm, 62 mm, 75 mm, 100 mm wide.

* **Flat wall brush** – sometimes called a distemper brush or a distemper flat. Different names are given to this brush depending on which part of the country you live in. Available in a wide range, varying in quality, including pure bristle which is quite expensive, costing about £30. The bristles are about 100 mm–150 mm long (the filling). There are cheaper ones available costing about £5. The fillings are man-made (50 mm–100 mm long).

  – Use: i) to apply emulsion paints to large areas

    ii) to apply adhesive to wallpapers.

  – Size: 100 mm, 125 mm, 150 mm, 175 mm wide.

* **Radiator** or **flag brush** – also called a funny tool, this brush has bristle fillings attached to a long wire handle which can be bent to fit into awkward areas such as radiators and behind pipes.

  – Size: 25 mm, 37 mm, 50 mm.

* **Crevice brush** or **bent fitch** – similar to a radiator brush and used to assist working in awkward places.

* **Fitch** – bristle filling is usually white and used to apply paint to detailed work and areas difficult to reach with paint brushes.

  – Size: flat or round 3 to 28 mm.

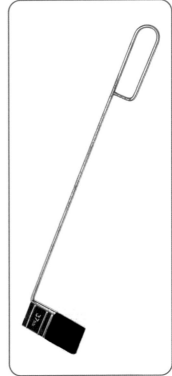

Radiator brush

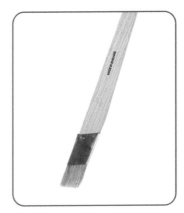

Fitch

TRY THIS

With advice from your tutor or supervisor, list some basic hand tools a painter and decorator may use. Other tradespeople could also use these tools. Add the list to your portfolio.

Wallpapering tools

Later in this chapter we will be looking at applying wallpaper. To apply wallpaper you will require basic paperhanger's tools and equipment. A basic paperhanging kit consists of:

* **Paste board (pasting table)** – made from wood or plastic, usually collapsible for easy transportation, and should be firm. Used for measuring, cutting, matching, pasting and folding wallpaper. Comes in various sizes, usually 1.830 m long x 560 mm wide.

* **Paperhanging brush** – made with a hardwood handle with pure bristle filling and used to apply wallpapers to the wall. Depending on what part of the country you come from you might find this called a sweep.

* **Caulker** – rigid plastic blade set in a wooden or plastic handle and used to apply wallpapers (also used as an alternative to a filling knife).

* **Trimming knives** – have retractable or snap-off blades and are used for trimming and cutting at angles and around obstacles.

* **Scissors or shears** – made of polished steel and used to cut lengths and trim at angles and around obstacles.

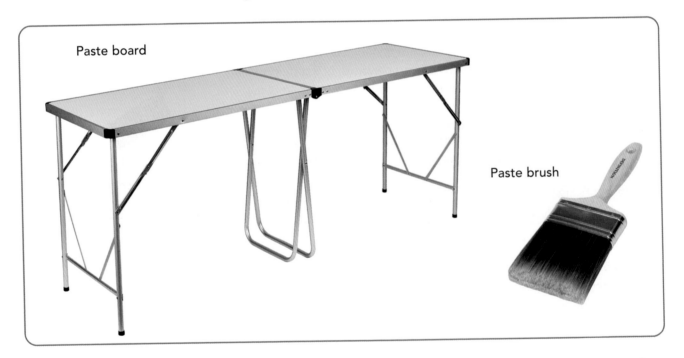

Paste board

Paste brush

* **Rule** – usually one metre long, constructed from four sections of boxwood or plastic. Used for measuring areas, lengths and widths.

* **Tape** – flexible metal strips of various lengths housed in plastic or metal casings. Used for measuring areas, lengths and widths.

* **Plumb bob and line** – a small weight suspended on a length of fine cord and used as a vertical guideline to ensure the first length of wallpaper on every wall is plumb.

* **Paste bucket** – made of plastic or galvanised iron and used for mixing wallpaper paste.

* **Paste brush** – see flat wall brush on page 173.

* **Pencil** – used to mark areas, lengths and widths.

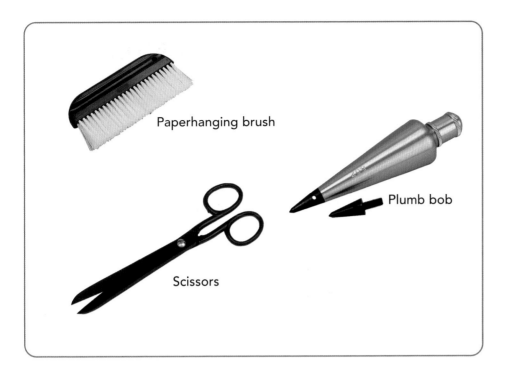

Paperhanging brush

Plumb bob

Scissors

Materials

You will use a variety of different materials as a painter and decorator, such as surface coatings (paints, varnishes and stains), adhesives and papers. Types of paint include:

* **Primer** – used to prepare new surfaces, such as metal and wood, for painting.

* **Undercoat** – a water- or solvent-based paint used to act as a first layer before applying the final overcoat. Undercoats help to even out the colour of the surface being painted and provide a good surface for the final paint layer/s.

* **Emulsion** – a water-based final paint that comes in several different finishes, such as matt, eggshell, soft sheen and silk.

* **Gloss finish** – a water- or solvent-based paint used for metalwork, plasterwork or woodwork.

We shall look in more detail at paints later.

Personal protective equipment

Prior to starting to do any painting and decorating job, you must first take into account any health and safety requirements for yourself and others. This includes using the appropriate PPE such as safety boots, bib and brace overalls, boiler suits, hand barrier cream, respiratory equipment and goggles.

TRY THIS

Make a list of personal protective equipment (PPE) required when preparing and decorating a room.

Water-based or solvent-based paints

In this section you will learn about...

* water-based paints

* solvent-based paints

* paint finishes

* preparing paint for use

* health and safety issues

* access equipment.

Paint is a liquid that dries to a hard finish and is applied to surfaces to enhance the appearance of such a surface. A **solvent** is a liquid used for thinning or dissolving something. The manufacture of paint is a complicated process. These are the basic ingredients:

* pigment – to give colour

* resin or oil – to make a coating adhere (stick) to the surface to provide gloss. It also provides resistance to water and chemicals

* thinner or solvent – to make the coating liquid enough to be easily and evenly applied to the surface

* driers – added to the paint to help it dry

* stabilisers – added to a paint to prevent lumps

* plasticisers – to prevent the paint from becoming too brittle when drying

* extenders – to make paints spread further

* anti-skinning agent – to prevent skin forming on the surface of the paint in the tin.

A sample of the huge range of paints available.

Water-based paints

These are thinned with water so you can wash brushes and rollers out in water.

There are three main types of water-based paint:

* **Matt emulsion paint** – used extensively on walls and ceilings. Suitable for plasterboard, hardboard, plaster and brick.

    - Spreading capacity: 60–65 m^2 per 5 litres on smooth, non-porous surface.

* **Vinyl silk emulsion paint/soft sheen** – used in the same way as matt emulsion but with a soft or high sheen. Note – for ease of cleaning, soft sheen is sometimes used on woodwork.

    - Spreading capacity: 60–65 m^2 per 5 litres on smooth, non-porous surface.

* **Acrylic primer/undercoat** – used for direct application on interior or exterior surfaces: new and old plaster, woodwork, concrete, building boards.

    - Spreading capacity: 65–90 m^2 per 5 litres.

Solvent-based paints

There are a number of solvent-based paints used but we will only look at the major types that you will use most often.

Oil-based wood primer (lead-free)

Used on interior and exterior woodwork, plywood, wallboards, medium density fireboard (MDF) and chipboard. All knots in woodwork should be sealed with patent knotting, which is a solution of shellac in methylated spirit. This material is used to prevent the resin from coming out of the knots in woodwork and softening and affecting the paint finish.

    - Thinner: white spirit.

    - Spreading capacity: 50–60 m^2 per 5 litres.

Undercoat (oil/resin undercoat)

A heavily pigmented paint which dries to a semi-matt finish. Designed for use under gloss paint. Used to provide body and colour to a paint system. Can be used over all suitably primed surfaces, inside and outside.

    - Thinner: white spirit.

    - Spreading capacity: 80–90 m^2 per 5 litres.

Eggshell or semi-gloss finish

An interior decorating finish which dries with a sheen. Also known as satin lustre or silk lustre finish. Used as a decorative finish for interior surfaces including ceilings, walls, woodwork and metalwork.

    - Thinner: white spirit.

    - Spreading capacity: 60–80 m^2 per 5 litres.

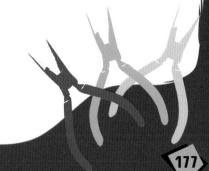

Gloss finish

Interior and exterior decorative paint which dries to a full gloss finish. Used as the main protective coating in the painting industry. Used for general interior and exterior finishes. Provides a decorative finish over suitably primed and undercoated surfaces.

– Thinner: white spirit.

– Spreading capacity: 75–85 m^2 per 5 litres.

EVIDENCE

With the help of your teacher or tutor or supervisor, and information from your paint supplier, list other types of paints used by a professional painter.

In a room in your school or college, measure the ceiling area and the wall area.

1. Calculate the amount of eggshell required for the ceiling. Use the information given about eggshell – two coats required.

2. Calculate the amount of gloss paint required for the wall areas. Use the information about gloss paint.

3. List the potential hazards in your practical work area.

4. List the access equipment used in the decorating industry.

Put the results into your portfolio.

Preparing paints for use

Paint must always be used from a kettle or tray, not direct from the manufacturer's containers. To pour paint from container to kettle or tray:

1. Remove any dust from the top of the container.

2. Open the lid, using the correct opener or a large screwdriver.

3. Stir the paint thoroughly with a mixing knife until all sediment is dispersed and a smooth consistency is achieved.

4. Pour the required quantity of paint into the kettle.

5. Brush away any paint on the rim or side of the container.

6. Replace the lid.

SAFETY TIP

Never use scrapers to open a paint tin as these can easily be bent.

Thinning

Many paints are supplied ready for application but some need thinning before use. These include:

* paints that are to be sprayed

* primers for absorbent surfaces (to ensure that they penetrate well)

* old paints that may have lost their thinners by evaporation and are too thick to be applied evenly and easily.

To thin such paints, add small quantities of the correct thinner until the required consistency is achieved. Always read the manufacturer's instructions before thinning.

Guide to use of thinners

Surface coating	Correct thinner
Oil-based Primers Undercoats Gloss and eggshell finishes Varnish glaze	White spirit
Water-based Emulsion paints Vinyl paints Acrylic primers and undercoats	Water
Spirit-based Wood stains Knotting French polish	Methylated spirit

Figure 9.1 Use of thinners

Paint strainers

Use a paint strainer to remove dirt, bits and skins from old paint. Some paints must be strained beforehand. Metal paint strainers have changeable gauze filters. Choose a filter of the correct mesh and ensure that it is securely clamped in the strainer.

Water paints   –   30 mesh

General use   –   40 mesh

Gloss   –   60 mesh

Use a brush to help the paint through the filter. Do not agitate the paint with a knife or stirrer, as this risks damaging the gauze.

Disposable paint strainers, made from stout paper and muslin, are suitable for small quantities of paint, but they should be used once and then thrown away.

Muslin, linen or nylon stocking stretched across the top of a paint kettle serve very efficiently as a means of straining small quantities of paint. They are easily replaced and present no cleaning problems.

Vacuum-assisted paint strainers really speed up paint filtering. They consist of a container and a lid which incorporates a venture jet and a large funnel with a detachable wire gauze filter. Compressed air blown through the jet creates a partial vacuum within the container, and paint is drawn through the filter at a remarkable speed.

Health and safety

You should always read the product safety information before using solvent-based paints. This information will be displayed on the side of the tin or can be supplied by the product manufacturer in the form of a Health and Safety Data Sheet.

Water-based paints are being used more these days as they cause fewer health, safety and environmental problems than solvent-based paints. However, this does not mean water-based paints are harmless; you must still follow the advice and guidance on the side of the tin and the Health and Safety Data Sheet.

Below is an example of the advice and guidance you will find on the side of a paint tin:

* Keep away from sources of ignition – no smoking.

* Lift with care.

* Ensure maximum ventilation during application and drying.

* Avoid contact with skin.

* Do not use white spirit to remove paint from skin.

* In case of contact with eyes, rinse immediately with plenty of water and seek medical advice.

* Before use, refer to the Safety Data Sheet.

Environmental issues

Always remove as much paint as possible from paint brushes and rollers before cleaning with a proprietary cleaner. Never empty waste liquid into drains. All waste paint and liquid should be disposed of using authorised disposal methods.

Access equipment

The majority of work a painter and decorator carries out is above ground level. Some of this work can be done at a normal working height without the assistance of access equipment, but a lot of the time during your working life you will be required to work at height. For this you will need to use access equipment.

There are various types of equipment that can assist you when required to work at height. The most common types are:

* ladders and stepladders

* trestle working platforms

* hop-ups

* scaffolding.

For this qualification you will only learn about stepladders and trestle working platforms. Remember, you will be responsible for putting up stepladders and trestle platforms, so you must ensure you know how to erect them and take them down safely. If you are unsure, ask for help. Dismantle and store access equipment safely when not in use.

Stepladders

These are mainly used for internal work but can be used outside as long as there is firm ground to stand them on, and you can open them out fully. Stepladders can be made out of timber or aluminium and come in various sizes and heights. They are made up of treads, reinforcing bars (on timber stepladders), cords (or a metal locking arm on aluminium steps), a back supporting frame and stiles.

Timber stepladders can be prone to damage, warping or twisting. Aluminium ladders are much lighter and stronger than timber ones, as well as being rot-proof.

Aluminium stepladder

Trestle working platform

Trestle working platforms consist of two trestles supporting a lightweight staging board between them. Folding trestles can also be made from either timber or aluminium and, as with stepladders, they must be fully extended before use. However, they are not to be used like a stepladder. Trestles should always be used in pairs with a lightweight staging board to work off. The advantage of trestles is that they form a quick, lightweight working platform which can easily be moved and re-erected where necessary.

Staying safe when using stepladders and trestle working platforms

These guidelines will help you keep safe when using access equipment.

1. Check stepladders, trestles and staging boards for damage before use.

2. Do not use them if they are broken, damaged, have been repaired or have missing parts.

3. Do not paint timber stepladders and trestles or use painted stepladders and trestles as the painting may hide defects .

4. Do not use aluminium ladders near overhead electric power lines.

5. If you find any defects on a piece of access equipment, report your findings immediately to your tutor, trainer or supervisor. A 'DO NOT USE' notice must be displayed on the item.

Trestle working platform

Preparing a room for decoration

In this section you will learn about...

* **how to prepare a room prior to decoration**

* **how to check the surfaces to see if they are in good condition**

* **how to prepare surfaces to receive a paint or paper finish**

* **health and safety.**

Preparation

Prior to starting any painting and decorating task, you must prepare the room ready for use. You cannot paint and decorate a room with all the furniture, pictures and curtains left in position. The correct sequence for preparing and decorating a room is:

1. Remove pictures and mirrors etc from the walls and store in a safe place.

2. Remove light furniture from the room.

3. Take down curtains and blinds from windows.

4. With help, move heavy furniture to the centre of the room.

5. Cover heavy furniture with dust sheets.

6. Cover the floor with dust sheets.

7. Place the decoration materials you are going to use on a dust sheet.

Checking condition of surfaces

Before you can begin painting, you need to assess the condition of the surfaces you are going to paint. It is rare that you can start painting existing surfaces without some sort of prior preparation, even if it is only washing to remove surface dust, dirt and grease. The presence of any or all of these will adversely affect the finish of your paint. At the beginning of any job, therefore, you should consider the following:

* What is on the ceiling (paint or wallpaper)?

* Is the ceiling dirty?

* Does the ceiling need filling?

* Does the ceiling need sanding?

* Does the wallpaper need removing from the ceiling?

* What is on the walls (paint or wallpaper)?

* Are the walls clean or dirty?

* Does the wallpaper need removing from the walls?
* Do the walls need washing or sanding?
* Do the walls need filling?
* What is on the woodwork?
* Is the woodwork clean or dirty?
* Does the woodwork need filling?
* Does the woodwork need sanding down?

TRY THIS

Look at a room that requires decorating.

1. Make a list of requirements prior to starting to decorate a room.

2. Assess the condition of all surfaces.

Preparation of surfaces

Prior to applying any material to any surface, it is essential that the surface is prepared to receive the paint or the wallpaper. There are two factors that will determine the type of preparation required before applying paint or wallpaper. If the surface is in good condition, the only preparation is to wash down and apply fresh paint. You may also have to **abrade** the area to obtain a key (grip) for paints to stick to. If the surface is not in good condition, you will have to **'make good'** by preparing the surface using filler and sanding down to achieve a level surface. If the surfaces have started to break down it will be necessary to completely remove the surface and get it re-plastered.

Abrade – to scrape or wear away by rubbing.

Make good – prepare a surface by using filler and sanding down to achieve a level surface.

TRY THIS

Look at areas in your school or college. Check the surfaces and list any areas that need to be 'made good'. Take photographs and notes and place them in your portfolio.

TRY THIS

Carry out this training task in your given training area.

Ask your tutor to allocate you a practical work area approx 3 m long and 2 m high, and if possible include a window frame or door frame, skirting boards and picture rail.

Prepare the area, 'make good' and apply two coats of matt emulsion paint.

Take a photo at each stage and place it into your portfolio.

Remember your PPE.

Nibs – fine particles left on the surface.

Preparatory and non-patterned wallpapers

In this section you will learn about...

❋ **different types of non-patterned wallpapers**

❋ **wallpaper pastes.**

Preparatory or lining wallpapers are used to hide defects in the wall prior to painting or applying finishing papers over the top. They are not patterned and can be made from various different materials. They can be painted over directly, or have a finish paper put over them. If they are to go under a finish paper, lining papers are often hung horizontally, rather than vertically, to avoid the edges of the lining paper and the finish paper falling in the same place.

Lining wallpapers

Lining papers are usually white, texture-free papers, rolled with the smoother face on outside. There are several types:

* basic lining paper

* reinforced, cotton- or linen-backed lining paper

* blown vinyl paper

* pitch paper.

◘ Basic lining paper

This is available in two qualities:

* White (W) to go under wallpaper.

* Extra White (XW) which is wood-free and more suitable for emulsion painting.

Size

The roll width dimension of lining paper is slightly wider than wallpaper 555 mm wide x 11 m long. Standard grade is also available in double, treble and quadruple length rolls. It is used to provide a surface of even porosity and to help mask surface irregularities.

Hanging

* Hang in opposite direction to the final wallpaper.

* Joints should be butted.

* Apply with stout starch or cellulose paste.

◘ Reinforced, cotton- or linen-backed lining paper

This is a heavy quality, white lining bonded to a fine cotton material. It is used on surfaces subject to excessive movement e.g. tongue and groove boarding or severely cracked plaster.

Size

10.5 m long x 530 mm wide.

Hanging

* Cotton side to the wall.

* Apply with stout paste.

Hanging wallpaper

🔁 Blown vinyl paper

This is a textured polyvinyl chloride (PVC) bonded paper that needs to be painted. It is used in both domestic and commercial properties.

Size

10.5 m long x 520 mm or 530 mm wide.

Hanging

* Apply with smoothing brush.

* Joints on internal or external angles should be overlapped.

* Apply with tub paste or cellulose paste.

🔁 Pitch paper

This is a brown lining paper which is coated with pitch – a dark, tarry substance that sets hard. It is used as a temporary barrier on walls that suffer from penetrating damp.

Size

10.5 m long x 555 mm wide.

Hanging

* Stout paste or special adhesive.

* Overlap joints to prevent moisture penetration through the joint.

Non-patterned wallpapers

These are finish wallpapers that have no coloured or repeating pattern. They include:

* woodchip or wood ingrain

* pulps

* vinyl.

British wallpaper

Distance around room (excluding doors and windows)

Wall Height	30 ft 9.1 m	34 ft 10.4 m	38 ft 11.6 m	42 ft 12.8 m	46 ft 14.0 m	50 ft 15.2 m	54 ft 16.4 m	58 ft 17.7 m	62 ft 18.9 m	66 ft 20.1 m	70 ft 21.3 m	74 ft 22.6 m	78 ft 23.9 m
8ft/2.5 m	5	5	6	7	7	8	9	9	10	10	11	12	12
9ft/2.75 m	6	6	7	7	8	9	9	10	10	11	12	12	13
10ft/3.05 m	6	7	8	8	9	10	10	11	12	13	13	14	15

Calculations based on roll measuring 20 in x 34ft or 52 cm x 10.3 m

American wallpaper

Distance around room (excluding doors and windows)

Wall Height	32 ft 9.7 m	36 ft 11.0 m	40 ft 12.2 m	44 ft 13.4 m	48 ft 14.6 m	52 ft 15.8 m	56 ft 17.1 m	60 ft 18.3 m	64 ft 19.5 m	68 ft 20.7 m	72 ft 21.9 m	76 ft 23.2 m	80 ft 24.4 m
8ft/2.5 m	8	9	10	11	12	13	14	15	16	17	18	19	20
9ft/2.75 m	9	10	11	12	14	15	16	17	18	19	20	21	22
10ft/3.05 m	10	11	12	14	15	16	17	19	20	21	22	23	25

Calculations based on roll measuring 18 in (when trimmed) x 24ft or 45.7cm x 7.3 m

Figure 9.2 Estimating the number of rolls

Woodchip or wood ingrain

This is the most common type of non-patterned wallpaper. It is a semi-relief wallpaper manufactured by placing small woodchips between a heavy backing paper and a thin surface paper. It is particularly used on walls or ceilings to hide surface defects. It can be painted over.

Size

10.05 m long x 520 mm or 530 mm wide.

Hanging

* Apply with stout paste.

* Joints should be butted.

Pulps

These are self-coloured papers used mainly in domestic properties. They are made from wood pulp and come in various qualities and thicknesses.

Size

10.05 m long x 520 mm or 530 mm wide.

Hanging

* Hang vertically.

* Apply with cellulose paste.

* Jointing should be butted.

Vinyl paper (non-patterned)

Most vinyl papers have a pattern on the surface, but there are non-patterned vinyl papers. These papers have a smooth or textured thin film of polyvinyl chloride (PVC) bonded to a backing and painted with (PVC) inks heat-fused on to the surface. Provides a washable surface. Used on surfaces which are subject to considerable handling and rubbing, or splashing and staining.

Size

10.5 m long x 520 mm or 530 mm wide.

Hanging

* Cellulose paste with anti-fungal properties.

* Joints should be butted.

* Use overlap adhesive if the paper has to be overlapped.

TRY THIS

Select the basic hand tools used to remove existing wallpapers and explain your choice. Place the results in your portfolio.

For each tool listed above, can you list the PPE you should use to protect yourself and others when it is being used?

The tables in Figure 9.2 (opposite) will help you to work out how many rolls you need for any particular job.

Pastes

Adhesives for decorative coverings are usually known as wallpaper pastes. They come in various forms:

* Powder or crystals, which are mixed with water to make paste.

* Ready-mixed in tubs.

* Ready-mixed in tubes.

When mixing up paste from powder or crystals, make sure you follow the manufacturer's instructions for the proportions of water to powder. Ensure it is mixed properly and is smooth. Remove any lumps before using or these will show through the paper.

Follow the manufacturer's instructions for how much paste you will need for your particular choice and amount of wallpaper.

Paperhanging terms

When wallpapering you must understand some basic terms:

* **Batch** or **shade number** – an identification number printed on a label inserted beneath the transparent cover. When you buy wallpaper check that all the numbers are the same.

* **Butt jointing** – the most common method of hanging wallpaper – the edges touch without overlap or gap.

* **Centring** – method of setting out a wall to avoid an unbalanced effect.

* **Concertina fold** – method of folding pasted covering to be applied to ceilings or horizontally to walls. Sometimes used when hanging very long lengths vertically (e.g. on staircases).

* **Cross-lining** – the hanging of lining paper horizontally.

* **End-to-centre folding** – pasting coverings which are hung vertically.

* **Plumb first length** – a guide to hang the first length of wallpaper so all lengths of paper are exactly vertical.

* **Roll** – the smallest unit by which wallpaper can be purchased.

* **Shading** – checking that each roll is exactly the same colour. Batch numbers must be the same.

* **Sizing** – the application of a thin coat of paste before hanging wallpaper.

* **Star cut** – the normal method of cutting wallpaper to fit around obstructions.

Hanging wallpaper

When you buy your wallpaper ensure that an extra roll with the same batch number will be available, otherwise if you need to buy more you may end up with a roll bearing a different batch number, and the colour shades may vary. Wallpaper should be hung on a sound, even, dry surface. Very poor surfaces may need re-plastering or, alternatively, you may have to cross-line with lining paper. Lining paper is hung to the wall the opposite way to the finishing paper. Some people hang lining paper to walls and then apply emulsion paint over the lining paper to give a flat, sound surface.

Establishing a vertical

Once you have decided on a starting position you need to establish a vertical so that the lengths of paper are correctly aligned.

Method

1. Measure out from the corner of the wall a distance that is 100 mm less than the full width of the paper and mark it top, middle and bottom.

2. Hang a plumb line from the top of the wall aligning with the mark nearest the corner and mark along it at intervals.

3. Join up the marks using a straight edge. This pencilled line is the vertical you will use for aligning the first length of paper.

4. The same process must be repeated each time a corner is turned.

Pasting

Some wallpapers are available pre-pasted, and only need wetting to activate the adhesive. But if you are pasting the paper yourself you will need a paste board (pasting table) on which to lay out lengths of paper. To avoid getting paste on the table, and consequently risk spoiling the next length of paper, some decorators let the paper overhang the table by 200 mm; however, it can be difficult to paste edges if they have no support. Keep a clean sponge and water handy and wipe away any paste which does get on to the paste board.

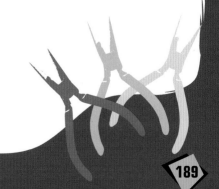

Most papers need to be left for a while to allow the paste to soak in and make the paper pliable. Papers with definite patterns should be pasted and hung one length at a time so that soaking times do not vary. A length of paper left too long will stretch irregularly and may not match the previous length.

Method

1. Apply paste down centre and work outwards. Fold pasted end in and paste second half.

2. Fold paper ends-to-centre and carry to the wall draped over your arm. Turn over ends of paper.

3. Position first length against pencilled vertical, over-lapping the ceiling by 50 mm and running to about 10 mm from the adjacent wall. Brush from the centre out.

4. Score along the ceiling line with the back of the scissors, peel the paper back and cut along the crease. Brush the paper back in place and repeat at skirting level.

TRY THIS

Try the method above, take a photograph and place the results into your portfolio.

TRY THIS

Ask your teacher or tutor to allocate you a wall area with an internal corner. You will also require a plumbbob and line, rule, pencil and a roll of wallpaper.

Measure the width of the wallpaper, reduce the width by 100 mm, take that measurement to the corner of the wall and place a pencil mark at the top, middle and bottom. Now drop your plumbline from the top of the wall, aligning with the mark nearest the corner, and mark it at intervals. Join up the marks using a straight edge. Ask your teacher or tutor to check your findings, take photographs and put in your portfolio.

Health and safety

Before hanging wallpaper you must follow various health and safety rules. The tools you will use when preparing and hanging wallpaper include some very sharp items which can cut you or others around you. When using scissors or shears do not leave them lying around on stepladders. Trimming knives are also very sharp. Always use a trimming knife with a retractable blade and never leave the blade exposed when not in use.

Some wallpaper adhesives contain fungicide solutions which stop mould growth but can be extremely harmful to you. Always read the instructions and guidance on the packet before use. You must always wash your hands after using this type of adhesive and avoid splashes to your eyes. If the adhesive gets into your eyes, rinse immediately with plenty of water and seek medical advice.

SAFE✚Y TIP

Remember to always wear suitable PPE when carrying out any painting and decorating task or disposing of waste liquids or materials.

EVIDENCE

It is now time for you to put what you have learnt into practice. In this section you will:

* select a range of basic hand tools

* identify solvent and water-based paints

* identify a range of PPE

* use brushes and rollers

* use hand tools to hang lining paper or wallpaper to straight walls

* clean the work area, tools and access equipment

* estimate approximately the quantity of materials required to carry out the task

* use good practice to erect and dismantle access equipment.

Ask your teacher or tutor to allocate you a practical work area approx 3 m long x 2 m high. If possible, include a window frame or door frame, skirting boards and picture rail.

1. Select the hand tools, brushes and rollers you will need and complete a requisition sheet.

2. Select the necessary PPE you will need to carry out the job (check with your teacher or tutor to make sure you are right).

3. Complete a risk assessment prior to starting the job.

4. Estimate the quantity of materials required to carry out the task.

5. Identify solvent- and water-based paints, select those most appropriate for the job and calculate how much you will need.

6. 'Make good' the surface.

7. Use hand tools to hang lining paper or wallpaper to straight walls.

8. Use brushes and rollers to apply paint to walls.

9. On completion, clean the work area, tools and access equipment.

*Remember to take care when cutting wallpaper.

Take photographs at each stage and put them in your portfolio.

Supplementary activities

1. List the tools and equipment used to hang wallpaper.

2. Obtain a sachet of paste and explain the mixing instructions to your teacher or tutor on a one-to-one basis.

3. Complete a risk assessment for applying wallpaper to a given area.

Ask your teacher or tutor to mark your results then put into your portfolio.

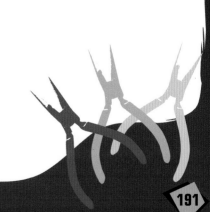

Developing building service skills

At the end of this unit you should be able to...

* recognise and select appropriate tools, materials and personal protective equipment (PPE) to carry out simple building services tasks

* apply safe working practices to the use of hand tools and equipment to perform basic mechanical services operations

* apply safe working practices to the use of hand tools and equipment to perform basic electrical operations.

10

Unit overview

This unit introduces you to the commonly used hand tools, equipment, components and craft skills required to perform basic plumbing and electrical operations. You will have the opportunity to position and secure plumbing and electrical components, and connect and test components under supervision.

It is assumed that you will either have successfully completed Unit 3: *Developing skills and working safely in construction* before starting this unit or that you will be studying Unit 3 alongside this unit. This unit is internally assessed. To pass you will complete a practical or written assignment set and marked by your teacher or tutor.

A building services professional at work.

What are plumbers and electricians?

In this section you will learn about...

* ❋ the work carried out by a plumber

* ❋ the work carried out by an electrician.

A **plumber** is a person who installs, repairs and maintains plumbing fixtures or systems in businesses, industries or residences. Plumbers generally work with a selection of components, including sanitary units, metal and plastic pipework and wastes, and ceramics to undertake many tasks. Their work can either be inside or outside domestic premises, factory units or businesses. Plumbers undertake various types of work relating to heating and gas systems. They may also specialise in leadwork. Plumbing is generally regarded as one of the mechanical services.

An **electrician** is a person who is directly involved in the installation, maintenance and repair of electrical services associated with buildings and structures. The work that they undertake may be in any type of building, such as houses, schools, offices, churches, factories, hospitals or shopping centres. Electricians may also undertake specialist tasks, including alarm systems, industrial work and maintenance of existing electrical infrastructure.

Electricians use a variety of different tools and equipment and work in the safest possible manner, as dealing with electricity can be extremely dangerous.

A plumber at work

Hand tools, materials and personal protective equipment (PPE)

In this section you will learn about...

* basic plumbing and electrical tools

* plumbing and electrical materials

* plumbing and electrical components

* PPE.

Basic plumbing and electrical tools

Any job in the construction industry requires the correct tools and equipment. A building services operative could be an electrical or a plumbing specialist, and both use a comprehensive range of tools. In this section we will look at the basic tools each of them needs to carry out their tasks.

We have included safety guidelines where appropriate. Some of these tools have already been described in earlier chapters, so refer back to these if necessary.

Saws

There are various types of saw available, and the type you choose should be related to the job needing doing.

Multi-purpose saw or panel saw – good for cutting relatively soft materials such as plastic. A multi-purpose saw of about 500 mm length is used for a high quality finish on all types of wood laminate and plastic pipe. It cuts on both the push and pull stroke. The advantage of using this type of saw when cutting plastic pipe is that the blade is large in area and therefore rigid, thus allowing you to make a straighter cut through the pipe (especially in waste pipe installations where the pipe is bigger than 30 mm in diameter).

Hacksaw – particularly useful for cutting metal. Two types of blade are commonly used, one having 22 teeth per 25 mm of blade length, and the other 32 teeth per 25 mm. The coarser blade (22) is used for steel pipe and the finer blade (32) for copper tube, although many plumbers use the smaller junior hacksaw for cutting the smaller sizes of copper tube, ducting and conduit.

Pipe cutters

In plumbing, there are a number of different types of pipe cutter used with different materials. You must ensure that you use the correct one for each specific task.

SAFE✛Y TIP

To make best use of a saw, the item to be cut should be secured in a vice. Hold the saw firmly by the handle and ensure that you keep your fingers well away from the blade.

Large hacksaw

SAFE✛Y TIP

When a hacksaw blade shows signs of wear, it should be replaced.

Snap-on pipe cutter

Burr – a rough edge or area left on material, such as metal, after it has been cast, cut or drilled.

Adjustable pipe cutter

Plastic-pipe cutter

Adjustable spanner

Snap-on pipe cutter – these operate by the rotation of a cutting wheel around the outside of the pipe. The wheel is gradually pushed through the pipe by a self-adjusting spring until the pipe is cut. Two sizes are available, for cutting 15 and 22 mm copper pipe. Snap-on pipe cutters are good for working in confined spaces. They are not suitable for stainless steel or plastic pipes.

Adjustable pipe cutter – similar to the snap-on pipe cutter but not self-adjusting. The wheel is gradually moved through the wall of the pipe by tightening it manually until the pipe is cut. The cutting wheel is narrow and sharp, but the cutting produces a **burr** around the inside edge of the pipe which must be removed by a reamer or round file. This type of cutter is suitable for copper, brass, aluminum and thin-walled steel tube with 15–45 mm diameter.

Plastic-pipe cutters – wherever possible always use these for cutting plastic pipe. It is important you use the right type of cutters for plastic pipe as it is much quicker and makes a 'cleaner' cut than a saw. This practice is recommended by manufacturers of plastic water-pipe systems. The use of pipe cutters will eliminate the risk of any particles of plastic being produced during the cutting process. This could cause problems if the particles found their way into the water-supply pipework.

Normally, when cutting plastic water-supply pipe with pipe cutters, you would not need to hold the pipe in a vice. This makes it a very simple and straightforward exercise. There are two main types of plastic-pipe cutter: blade type and pliers type. Read the manufacturer's instructions for both types to check if the pipe should be rotated when cutting.

Staying safe when using pipe cutters

* Always follow manufacturer's instructions.

* Do not put your fingers anywhere near the blade.

* Do not use excessive force with a pipe cutter. This can permanently damage it, making it unfit for use and potentially dangerous.

There are no maintenance requirements for these tools, and the blade should last a long time, but once it fails to cut cleanly, replace the item.

Spanners

Spanners are available in a variety of types. The most common are:

* adjustable

* open-ended

* ring

* box.

Adjustable spanner – available in several sizes and designs, and most plumbers include at least two different lengths in their tool kit. Adjustable spanners are most suitable for assembly and disconnection work to pipework and components.

Open-ended spanner – usually, but not always, double-ended, with each end taking a different sized nut. They are described by the size of the thread on which the nut screws, or by the distance across the flats of the nut.

Ring spanner – fits completely round the nut to hold it very securely. Ring spanners are safer to use than open-ended spanners as there is less risk of the spanner slipping off the nut. Also they are less likely to wear or open out. They are preferred for jobs where the nuts must be tightened more securely.

Box spanner – most useful for releasing or tightening recessed nuts in inaccessible positions such as those securing taps to wash basins, baths and sink units. Most box spanners are double-ended and are turned by a steel rod called a tommy bar.

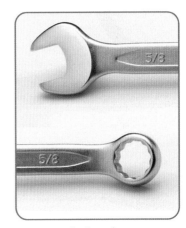

Open-ended and ring spanners

⬆ Pipe grips or wrenches

There are five main types of wrenches used in plumbing:

* Stillson

* footprint wrench

* chain wrench

* self-grip wrench

* basin wrench.

Stillson – a very robust tool that is most suitable for steel pipe. Stillsons are available in a wide variety of lengths, ranging from 150 mm to 1.225 m. The most adaptable sizes for plumbers' work are 250 mm and 450 mm.

Footprint wrench – relies on handgrip pressure to secure the pipe or component. These are available in lengths ranging from 150 mm to 400 mm.

Chain wrench – also called chain tongs. This is usually associated with industrial work, but small models are available for domestic purposes. The length of the lever handle can vary between 200 mm and 900 mm.

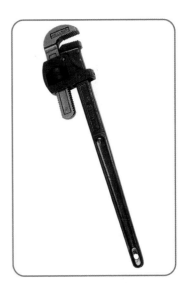

Stillson pipe wrench

Self-grip wrench – relies on hand pressure to secure the component, although self-grip wrenches also have a lock-on action to securely grip the wrench on to the component, allowing the grip pressure to be released. They are available with jaws of alloy steel and in lengths from 150 mm to 250 mm.

Self-grip wrench

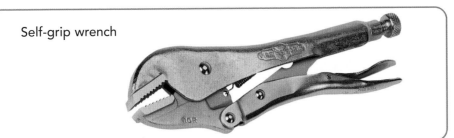

197

Basin wrench

Basin wrench – designed for difficult jobs such as fitting **backnuts** and **union nuts** behind wash basins, baths and sink units. Basin wrenches can be used in the vertical or horizontal position, enabling a nut to be tightened or loosened in the most inaccessible places. Basin wrenches are approximately 250 mm long and fit standard size backnuts.

Backnut – a locking nut provided on the screwed shank of a tap, valve or pipe fitting for securing it to some other object. It is a threaded nut, dished on one face to retain a grommet, used to form a watertight joint on a long threaded connector.

Union nut – a screwed pipe fitting, usually brass or low carbon steel. It enables pipes or appliances to be quickly connected or disconnected.

Files and rasps

Hand file – used to shape material by abrasion. A file typically takes the form of a hardened steel bar, mostly covered with a series of sharp, parallel ridges or teeth. Files normally have a narrow, pointed **tang** at one end on to which a handle can be fitted. Files come in a wide variety of sizes, shapes and tooth configurations. The cross-section of a file can be flat, round, half-round, triangular, square, or of a more specialised shape. A file's teeth can range from rough, coarse and bastard (meaning intermediate) to second-cut, smooth and dead smooth.

Rasp – similar to a file, but the cutting surface is coarser and can quickly and effectively smooth off the rough edges of softer materials. It is used particularly to smooth and remove rough edges from plastic. You should use both hands when using a rasp, one on the handle and the other at the front edge.

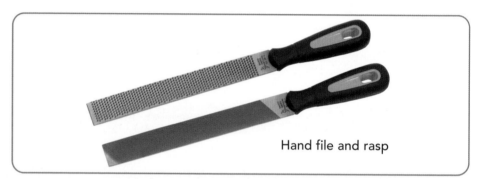

Hand file and rasp

Staying safe when using files and rasps

* Be careful of the sharp handle of a file.

* Never use a hammer with a file.

* If the handle on a rasp is loosened or absent, do not use it as you run a high risk of injury to your hand.

* Rasps are hard-wearing and last a long time, but when they show signs of wear they should be replaced.

* Use both hands when working with a rasp.

* Use eye protection PPE when using rasps, as the fine particles of material could cause serious damage to your eyes.

* If requested, use a face mask when using files as there is a risk of inhaling dust particles.

Rules and measures

Steel ruler – constructed from steel or stainless steel and comes in lengths from 150 mm to 1 metre long.

Tape measure – Flexible metal strips of various lengths housed in plastic or metal casings and used to measure materials and areas.

🗹 Pipe benders

Bending spring – used to bend copper pipes. It is designed to prevent the pipe from collapsing during the bending process. Bending springs can be used externally or internally.

Bending machines – work on the principle of leverage and can be either hand held (hand bender) for tubes up to 22 mm, or free-standing (stand bender) for tubes up to 42 mm.

🗹 Blow-torch

A blow-lamp or blow-torch is an important part of a plumber's tool kit. You can get both small and large blow-torches. They are fuelled by liquefied petroleum gas (LPG), most commonly propane.

🗹 Staying safe when using a blow-torch

* Wear the recommended PPE, usually goggles or a visor and gloves.

* Do not use a blow-torch until you have received training.

* Make yourself fully aware of the safety issues involved in using highly inflammable LPG.

* Read manufacturer's instructions carefully.

* Be particularly careful when using a blow-torch in the vicinity of combustible materials such as timber and polythene pipe.

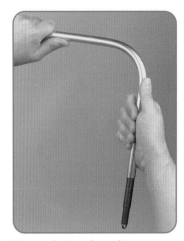

Internal pipe-bending spring

Blow-torch

TRY THIS

1. Identify and list the blow-torch equipment shown in Figure 10.1.

2. Produce a list detailing the assembly procedure for the equipment shown below.

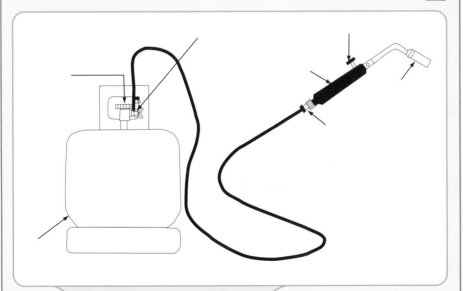

Figure 10.1 Blow-torch.

Record your findings and ask your teacher or tutor to mark them and put your answers into your portfolio.

Hydraulic pressure tester

A test for leaks is carried out on sections of completed hot and cold water pipework. A hydraulic pressure tester forces water into the system and measures the water pressure.

Screwdrivers

As there are many different types of screw, there are many different types of screwdriver. The main defining characteristic of a screwdriver is its tip. The commonest screwdriver is the slotted screwdriver. This has a flat, slightly tapered tip like a blade. Slotted screws are found everywhere, even on electronics. The straight shape means that you have to look at the screw to place the screwdriver – you can't easily do it by 'feel' – and the bevelled design means that the driver has a tendency to slip out of the slot when turned. Slotted screwdrivers are measured across the width of the tip in either inches or millimetres.

Other screwdrivers are the cross-headed Phillips® screwdriver, and the similar Posidriv® screwdriver. See page 117–118 for more on these types.

Pliers and cutters

These are essential tools to an electrician. The pliers that an electrician uses must have insulated handles for comfort and protection from shock and live power sources. They come in different sizes and all have different uses e.g. needle nose pliers, round nosed pliers, long nosed pliers. Wire cutters also must have insulated handles to prevent shock from potential live cables.

Wire strippers

Wire strippers are used to accurately strip the protective insulation from around the cables. These come in a variety of adjustable diameters to strip insulation on cables of different thicknesses.

Tin snips

Tin snips are strong shears that will cut different metals. Plumbers mainly use these to cut lead for external weatherproofing, gutters and flashings on chimney work.

Pliers

Cutters

Tin snips

Wire strippers

Hammers

Building services workers use a selection of hammers in their everyday tasks. The most common hammers are ball hammers used to shape metal and rivets, and claw hammers for general use, lifting floor boards and de-nailing timber. See page 116 for more on hammers.

Wire wool

Wire wool, or steel wool, is used by plumbers for general-purpose cleaning of copper pipe and fittings, and paint removal. It is available in the following grades: 000 (extra fine), 00 (fine), 1 (medium) and 3 (coarse). A medium grade is normally used.

Sheet metal formers

Sheet metal formers are used to provide a surface against which a material is beaten and moulded into a shape. The most common sheet metals used are lead and copper when constructing flashings and waterproof coverings for roofs, chimneys and canopies. They can also be used for guttering and external features to houses. Generally sheet metal formers are made from timber.

Craft knives

Craft knives are used to accurately cut pieces of textile, plastic, plywood, metals etc. that may be too flimsy to cut with a more robust tool. The handles are made of plastic, aluminium or steel and can sometimes have additional grip for comfort. They can have adjustable, retractable blades and locking devices to lock the blade into position.

Craft knife

Grips

Grips, also occasionally known as mole grips, are used to hold work or equipment securely in place. They are made from an alloy steel and have a screw for adjustment, and a quick release trigger incorporated into the handles.

Plumbing and electrical materials

Copper pipe

Copper pipe is available in sizes ranging from 6 mm to 159 mm diameter.

Mole grips

It comes in four grades: W, X, Y and Z. The basic difference between the grades of pipe is the wall thickness and **temper**. The outside diameter of pipe always remains the same.

* Grade X is for general-purpose plumbing work – the most commonly used.

* Grade Y is softer, thicker-walled, and usually supplied in coils.

* Grade Z is hard tempered with thin walls, and is unbendable.

* Grade W is used for **microbore** heating systems.

Microbore – copper pipe with diameters of 8 mm and 10 mm.

Temper – the degree of hardness in a metal.

Copper tubing of difference grades

Jointing paste

Thread tape

Tub of flux

Potable water – water that is fit for humans to drink.

SAFE✛Y TIP

NEVER use your finger to apply flux. ALWAYS use a brush.

Oxidisation – a chemical reaction between a substance – particularly a metal, such as copper or iron – with oxygen, forming a new compound called an oxide. Rust, for instance, is iron oxide.

⬭ PVC (Polyvinyl chloride) pipes

PVC is one of the most common pipework materials. It is used for discharge and drainage pipework. PVC is cheap and easy to assemble. It has been used extensively in a wide range of construction products for over 50 years. PVC's strong, lightweight, durable and versatile characteristics make it ideal for pipes and fittings. It is easy to handle and transport, and is used for guttering and downpipes as well as fittings and drainage.

PVC is an alternative to high-density polyethylene (HDPE) for water, gas and land drainage pipe. PVC pipe can be joined together in a number of different ways, including pushfit and solvent welded (glued) fittings for all diameters, as well as multi-fit (mechanical) fittings for 32 mm, 40 mm and 50 mm waste pipe.

⬭ Sealing joints

Jointing paste (compound) – produces a leakproof seal on all types of metal and plastic threading connections. It should be brushed liberally on to the male threads of the joint before assembly.

Jointing compound remains plastic indefinitely on hot or cold pipes and won't shrink, crumble or crack. It ensures tight joints and prevents fittings freezing to threads. Jointing compound is designed especially for use with hot and cold **potable** water.

Thread tape – a thin white tape used to wrap the threaded ends of pipes to make the joint watertight. It is used when making joints on water and steam pipes.

Solder – lead-free wire for fusing copper-pipe connections when heated with a blow-torch. It is highly effective, designed to produce perfect joints quickly and cleanly. You need to use flux with solder.

Flux – a white compound required when soldering to prevent **oxidisation** of the joint. Flux helps molten solder to wet, adhere to and alloy with the copper tube.

The manufacturer's advice should always be followed prior to use. Modern fluxes, especially the self-cleaning types, can be more aggressive to the copper tube and need to be used with extreme care. Excess use of flux causes increased rates of corrosion of the pipework. Flux should NOT be applied to the fittings. A thin coating should be applied to the outside of a cleaned tube with a brush. Always wipe off the excess flux.

TRY THIS

Look around your school or college and research the areas where plastic pipes and copper pipes are used.

1. List the uses you have found and the areas where they are used.

2. List the advantages and disadvantages of plastic and copper pipework.

Ask your teacher or tutor to check your findings and insert your notes into your portfolio.

⬚ Insulated cable

Cables must have their conductors separated from each other to avoid contact and possible fire. They must be segregated and protected by insulation to avoid them touching any other materials or surrounding metalwork. The materials that can be used to insulate the cable are:

* PVC

* magnesium oxide

* silicon rubber

* synthetic rubbers.

PVC – the most common insulator. It is a good option as it is robust, flexible and cheap. It is adaptable to work with and easy to install. Its only downside is that it will not withstand extremes of heat and cold.

Magnesium oxide – magnesium oxide is a white powder used as an insulator for mineral-based insulated cables (MICC). This type of insulation absorbs moisture, and care must be ensured to avoid dampness. A special seal, called a termination gland, is used at the end of the cable to stop any moisture from passing through into it. This cable is fireproof and anti-corrosive. Mineral cables are copper-sheathed, and this enables them to withstand a certain degree of mechanical force. They are also able to withstand high temperatures.

Silicon rubber – a popular cable for wiring to fire alarm systems as it has aluminum over-sheath foil. The FP200 rubber silicon cable retains insulation properties after it is heated up, and this is now a cheaper option than mineral insulated, metal-sheathed cables.

Synthetic rubbers – can withstand high temperatures better than PVC and are therefore used for the main connections of immersion heaters, storage heaters and equipment used in boilerhouses.

SAFE✚Y TIP

PVC insulation should never be burned from the cable as it gives off dangerous toxic fumes.

Components

⬚ Copper pipe fittings

The three most widely used types of fittings for jointing copper tubes are:

* soldered capillary joints

* push-fit joints

* integral solder ring fitting

* end feed fitting

* compression joints.

We will look at the last three.

Integral solder ring fitting – can be used for above- and below-ground work. It is used extensively in construction, gas, water and engineering pipelines conveying air and water. It is an extremely attractive fitting and is also easy to make. The above points make this type of fitting the most popular, and best known, of all capillary fittings.

Integral solder ring fitting

End feed fitting

Compression fitting

S, P and bottle traps

The integral solder ring fitting relies on the phenomenon of **capillary attraction** in making the joint. Each fitting contains the correct amount of solder as an integral part. When heat is applied, the solder turns from a solid to a liquid and is drawn by capillary attraction around the whole joint in the tight space between the outside of the pipe and the inside of the fitting.

End feed fitting – used in exactly the same circumstances as for the integral solder ring fittings, and is identical in all ways except that the solder has to be added to the end of the fitting.

Compression joints – use a nut and compression ring. They require the end of the tube to be cut square and to length. The nut is then slipped over the tube end followed by the compression ring (olive) and then tightened up with an adjustable spanner.

TRY THIS

Bends and tee pieces are exactly the same size, so you may find it helpful to dismantle one fitting and use this as a 'template' or guide in the course of your assembly work. You could use this when taking your centre-to-centre measurements of sections of pipe before measuring the final dimensions.

Conduits

Conduits are plastic or steel tubes that offer protection to cables from mechanical damage. They enable a system to be rewired without damaging any plastered or decorative finishes.

Trunking

Trunking is similar to conduit but it is surface-mounted on the face of walls. It is fitted with a removable cover, which can be snapped on. Trunking is used as both protection to the cables and also to conceal them and to provide a more pleasing finish.

TRY THIS

List as many different electrical appliances or services you can find that your school or college uses every day.

Plastic waste traps

Traps are used on above-ground discharge system pipework and appliances. Their function is to retain a 'plug' of water to prevent foul air from the sanitation and drainage pipework entering the room. Traps are mainly manufactured in plastic (polypropylene to B.S.3943), although they are also available in brass for use on copper pipework, where a more robust installation is required. They can be chromium-plated to provide a pleasing appearance. Waste traps come in three basic designs:

* P
* S
* bottle.

Waste pipe fittings

Manufacturers of waste pipework systems provide a very comprehensive range of fittings to suit all pipe sizes. Most of the fittings are available in all of the types mentioned above. The finished end of manufactured lengths of pipe has a narrower chamfered edge. The chamfer allows the plumber to push the fitting on to the pipe end. If you have to cut a short length of pipe, the cut end will not have a chamfer. You will need to form the chamfer yourself with a rasp.

Pillar taps

Pillar taps come in various styles and models. They have a long vertical thread that passes through pre-drilled holes in an appliance. They are secured by a back nut and the feed pipe is then connected.

Socket outlets (13A rated)

Electrical socket outlets can be single or double, switched or unswitched, and are usually surface or flush mounted. Some socket outlets have neon indicator lights to show if the source is switched on. Sockets are positioned at different heights as follows:

* For general use they are placed a minimum of 450 mm above the floor.

* For elderly and disabled people they are placed between 825 mm and 900 mm above the floor and 1200 mm over work surfaces.

Light fittings

Lighting circuits generally consist of lamp holders and switches. Lamp holders are usually wall or ceiling mounted; they can also be pendant (suspended from the ceiling) with one or more lamp- or tube-holders. Switches are generally 6 amp plate switches and come in double or two-gang, pullcord or dimmer types. In bathrooms you must always use pullcord as it is a high-risk area where moisture is present.

Tungsten lamps

Early **incandescent** lamps used to be made from a carbon filament enclosed in a glass tube from which air had been partially removed. The concern usually was that at high temperatures the carbon would break down and cause the inside of the glass envelope to blacken. Nowadays tungsten is used as it has a higher melting point than carbon.

General lighting service (GLS) lamps – these are standard lamps commonly known as 'light bulbs', although bulb really only refers to the glass that surrounds the inner components of the lamp. GLS lamps come in wattages of 25 W to 2000 W. They consist of a coiled tungsten filament inside a glass bulb. The coiled filament allows internal convection currents to be produced as the lamp heats up, enabling the filament lamp to run at a higher temperature because it cools itself. There are also double-coiled filaments which increase the cooling effect. To reduce the rate of loss of the filament when burning, a mixture of nitrogen and argon is used inside the lamp. GLS lamps have two types of fitting to connect to the supply: bayonet cap (BC) and Edison screw (ES or GES).

Residual current device (RCD)

A residual current device automatically disconnects the power supply if there is a sudden surge of current, or if there appears to be an earthing fault in the system.

Waste fitting

Electrical socket

Incandescence – glowing light created by heat.

Residual current device

Cartridge fuse

Cartridge fuses

Cartridge fuses are used to protect sensitive equipment from overcurrent. They are made from porcelain tubes filled with granular silica. They have metal end caps to which an element is attached. The two main types of fuse are:

* B.S.1362

* B.S.1361.

B.S.1362 – commonly found in domestic plug tops. This usually has a fuse rating of either 3 amp or 13 amp. The 3 amp is commonly found in radios, table lamps or anything up to 720 watts. The 13 amp should be present in all appliances of 720 watts or over e.g. kettles, toasters, lawnmowers, washing machines etc.

B.S.1361 – normally used in distribution boards and main intake positions.

Prior to selecting a fuse for an appliance, you must consult a qualified electrician who will give you advice on correct cartridge selection.

SAFE✚Y TIP

Look again at Unit 3: *Developing skills and working safely in construction*

Health and safety

Before you start any building services job, you must first take into account any health and safety requirements for yourself and others.

TRY THIS

Make a list of personal protective equipment (PPE) required when undertaking plumbing or electrical tasks.

case study

Charlie is an apprentice with a small construction company. She is learning about all aspects of construction work but wants to become an electrician. She has been asked to help an experienced electrician to carry out repairs to an electrical ventilation system on the outside of a four-storey building. She arrives for the job early, before her supervisor, and is keen to impress him so organises all the PPE and tools she thinks they will need for the job.

Questions and activities

1. List the tools and equipment Charlie and her supervisor will need.

2. List the PPE Charlie and her supervisor should wear.

3. What sort of access equipment do you think they might use to do the job?

4. If Charlie's supervisor doesn't turn up, what should Charlie do?

Mechanical services operations

In this section you will learn about...

* **joining and bending of copper pipe**

* **connection of pipework to sinks**

* **ductwork.**

Jointing tasks

In the following section we shall look at some straightforward mechanical services operations, including two methods of jointing copper tubing. There will then be opportunities for you to try out some practical tasks, including bending copper pipework and connecting pipework to sinks.

The two jointing operations are:

* capillary fitting assembly

* compression assembly.

Capillary fitting assembly

1. Select a piece of copper piping.

2. Cut the tube square.

3. De-burr or file the end of the tube.

4. Clean the outside of the tube.

5. Clean the inside of the fitting.

6. Sparingly apply flux to each surface.

7. Push the tube all the way into the fitting.

8. Apply heat until the solder melts.

9. Ensure the solder has completely run.

10. Once the solder has run, remove the heat.

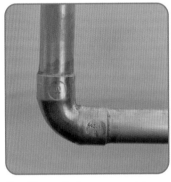

Capillary fitting assembly

Compression assembly

Cut the tube to the required length, using either a junior hacksaw or pipe cutters.

1. De-burr the inside of the pipe (if cut with pipe cutters) or the inside and outside of the pipe (if cut with a hacksaw).

2. Place the nut and compression ring on to the pipe.

3. This process is applied to each pipe end being used in the fitting (two for a straight coupling or elbow, three for a tee).

Compression fitting
assembly

4. Assemble the fitting. The joint should be finger tight, with all the fitting components fully engaged.

5. Tighten the fitting using adjustable grips or spanners.

TRY THIS

Activity 1: Copper tube framework

After a practical demonstration by your teacher or tutor of measuring, cutting, bending and jointing copper tube, you will be expected to fabricate the copper tube framework shown in Figure 10.2.

1. Produce a list of pipe and fittings you will require to carry out the work.

2. Select tools and equipment you will require.

3. Correctly measure, mark out and cut the pieces of tube required.

4. Fabricate the bends.

5. Join the lengths of 15 mm copper tube using soldered and compression fittings.

6. Test the completed installation to 3 bar for 3 minutes. All joints and pipe should be leak-free.

7. Decommission on completion.

NOTE:
Tolerance + or – 2 mm, all pipe ends to be de-burred

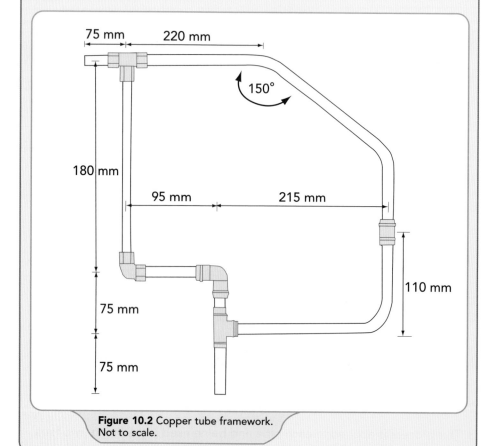

Figure 10.2 Copper tube framework.
Not to scale.

EVIDENCE

For *Try This* Activity 1:

1. Take a photograph of the completed pipework and put it into your portfolio.

2. Put the list of pipes and fittings into your portfolio.

Ask your teacher or tutor to mark your results and put them into your portfolio.

EVIDENCE

From your material list from *Try This* Activity 1, calculate the following costs for the completed task:

15 mm compression tees	@ £2.41 each
15 mm compression elbows	@ £1.66 each
15 mm copper tube	@ £2.17 per metre
15 mm capillary copper elbows	@ £0.53 each
15 mm capillary copper connectors	@ £0.30 each
15 mm copper tees	@ £0.99 each

Total £

Discount the total by 10 %

Discounted total £

Add 17.5 % VAT to the discounted total

Final cost £

Ask your teacher or tutor to check your findings, and insert your findings into your portfolio.

Now we can move on to the sink unit pipework exercise. The skills you have picked up when working with copper pipes and fittings in Activity 1 should prove useful for this next task.

TRY THIS

Activity 2: Copper pipe installation to sink unit

After a practical demonstration by your teacher or tutor of measuring, cutting, bending and jointing copper tube, carry out the following with reference to Figure 10.3.

1. Produce a list of pipe and fittings you will require to carry out the work.

2. Select the tools and equipment you will require.

3. Correctly measure, mark out and cut the pieces of tube required.

4. Fabricate the bends.

5. Join the lengths of 15 mm and 22 mm copper tube using soldered and compression fittings.

6. Test the completed installation to 3 bar for 3 minutes. All joints and pipe should be leak-free.

7. Decommission on completion.

NOTE:
Tolerance + or – 2 mm, all pipe ends to be de-burred.
22 mm pipe to be joined using compression fittings.
15 mm pipe to be joined using capillary fittings.

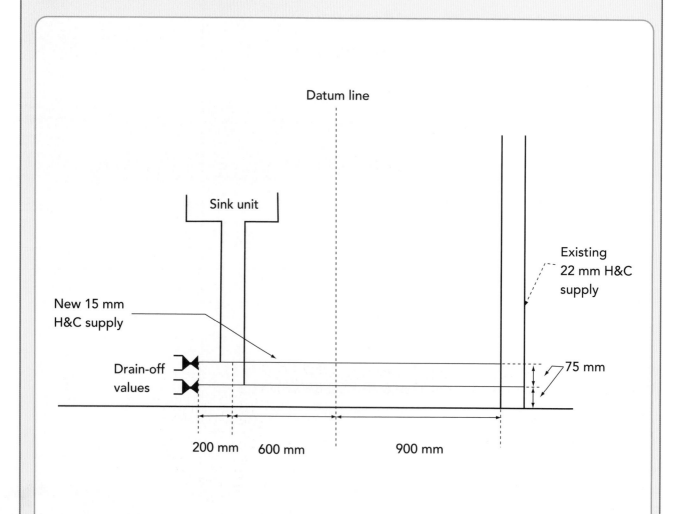

Figure 10.3 Copper pipe installation to sink unit. Not to scale.

EVIDENCE

From your material list for *Try This* Activity 2, calculate the following costs for the completed task:

22 mm x 22 mm x 15 mm compression tee	@ £1.66 each
15 mm copper tube	@ £0.76 per metre
15 mm copper elbows	@ £0.53 each
15 mm copper connectors	@ £0.30 each
15 mm copper tees	@ £0.99 each
15 mm drain-off valves	@ £1.12
15 mm capillary tap connectors	@ £2.55
15 mm clips	@ £ 0.07 each
22 mm copper tube	@ £4.25 per metre
22 mm clips	@ £ 0.10 each

Total £

Discount the total by 10 %

Discounted total £

Add 17.5 % VAT to the discounted total

Final cost £

Ask your teacher or tutor to check your findings, and put them into your portfolio.

EVIDENCE

For *Try This* Activity 2:

1. Take a photograph of your finished installation and put it into your portfolio.

2. Put the list of pipes and fittings into your portfolio.

Ask your teacher or tutor to mark your results, and put them into your portfolio.

Activity 3: Plastic waste pipe to sink unit

After a practical demonstration by your teacher or tutor of measuring, cutting and jointing plastic soil and waste pipe, carry out the following with reference to Figure 10.4.

1. Produce a list of pipe and fittings you will require to carry out the work.

2. Select tools and equipment you will require.

3. Correctly measure, mark out, cut and drill the soil pipe, and insert the boss connections and branch pipes as shown on the drawing.

4. Correctly measure, cut and connect waste pipe and fittings to sink unit waste.

5. Decommission on completion.

NOTE:
Tolerance + or – 2 mm

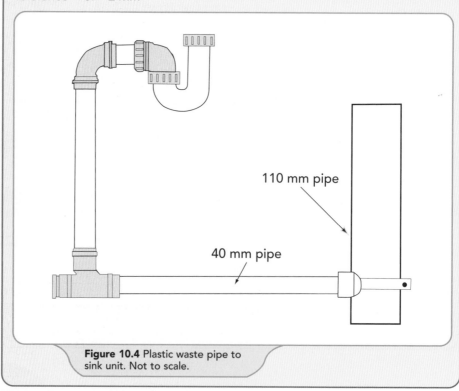

110 mm pipe

40 mm pipe

Figure 10.4 Plastic waste pipe to sink unit. Not to scale.

Ducting/trunking

Trunking or ducting is a prefabricated casing which covers cables en route to their systems. Trunking may be hinged, which can then allow access to repair or maintain services. Trunking is frequently used in factories and outlets as it can be easily accessed to modify, relocate or simply remove pieces of equipment.

Trunking can be plastic or steel, depending on the nature of use, and can be determined by its location. The range of types can be square, floor, multi-compartment, flush, overhead or skirting trunking. If used outside, adequate care must be ensured to protect against atmospheric conditions.

Basic electrical operations

In this section you will learn about...

* **electrical supply**

* **light fittings**

* **ring main wiring**

* **isolation and testing.**

Basic electrical theory

The following notes are information needed for the practical tasks that you will now undertake. Read the notes then carry out the tasks.

Electrical supply

The electrical supply within the United Kingdom is delivered by a number of supply authorities. These include npower, ScottishPower, Powergen, Nuclear Electric and other companies. The electrical supply that goes mainly to buildings is 230 volt single-phase or 400 volt three-phase.

The supply must have:

* sufficient earthing to prevent shocks to the occupiers

* sufficient precautionary measures in place to prevent the outbreak of fire

* sufficient measures in place to combat against current leakage.

All supplies these days go straight into an energy meter. If anything goes wrong with the electrical source or supply, this is the point that electricity suppliers will normally repair up to. Energy meters are usually installed on the outside of newer properties in lockable boxes. This is the preferred method for most suppliers, as it is secure, and it is easier to take a meter reading if the occupier is not in the property.

Lighting circuits

Lighting circuits have a variety of switch arrangements. These can be one-way, two-way or intermediate switch control. One-way switch control is the most basic form of control, with a one-way switch controlling one light. Sometimes we need to switch a light on from more than one location, for instance at the top and bottom of a staircase. This is where we would use two-way switch control.

Lighting circuit wiring systems commonly use the **loop-in method**. In domestic situations this is by far the most popular method, using a twin and earth (PVC/PVC/CPC) cable. In loop-in circuits, power is fed from the consumer unit to the first light and then to each consecutive light on the circuit. More than one

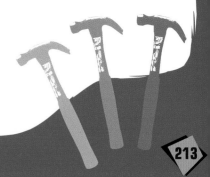

lighting circuit should be used for each installation so that in the event of a circuit lighting failure, some of the lighting would still be in good working order.

No more than 100 watts per outlet should be used as this may otherwise overload the circuit.

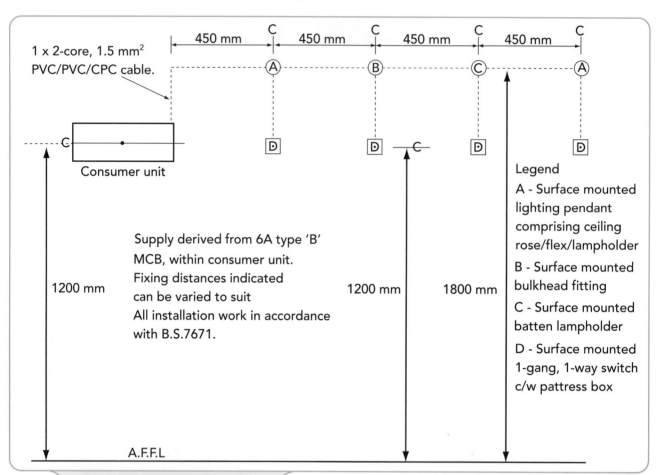

1 x 2-core, 1.5 mm² PVC/PVC/CPC cable.

Consumer unit

Supply derived from 6A type 'B' MCB, within consumer unit. Fixing distances indicated can be varied to suit
All installation work in accordance with B.S.7671.

Legend
A - Surface mounted lighting pendant comprising ceiling rose/flex/lampholder
B - Surface mounted bulkhead fitting
C - Surface mounted batten lampholder
D - Surface mounted 1-gang, 1-way switch c/w pattress box

Figure 10.5 Loop-in lighting sub-circuit with 1-way switch control.

⚛ Consumer power supply control unit

This is still commonly called a fusebox because older units contain fuses as a way to isolate the supply if there is a sudden surge of power. Modern consumer units are made up of **miniature circuit breakers** (MCBs) attached to the live or phase bar. They also have additional protection with a split load **residual current device** (RCD) that can be used to power any equipment outside the premises.

Ring circuits

In a domestic ring circuit the phase, neutral and circuit protective conductors are connected to their respective terminals within the consumer unit, and are looped to each socket outlet in turn before returning back to the consumer unit, thus forming a ring.

To protect against overcurrent a 32 amp protective device is used. The number of socket outlets connected to the ring is unlimited within a floor area not exceeding 100 m² .

Triple-pole MCB

Miniature circuit breaker (MCB) – an automatic switch that opens when too much current flows through the circuit, effectively cutting off the electricity supply and preventing any damage to the circuit. The MCB is undamaged by the operation, and when the switch is closed again the current returns to normal.

Residual current device (RCD) – a device that monitors the current flowing in phase and neutral conductors, and cuts off supply if an earth fault occurs.

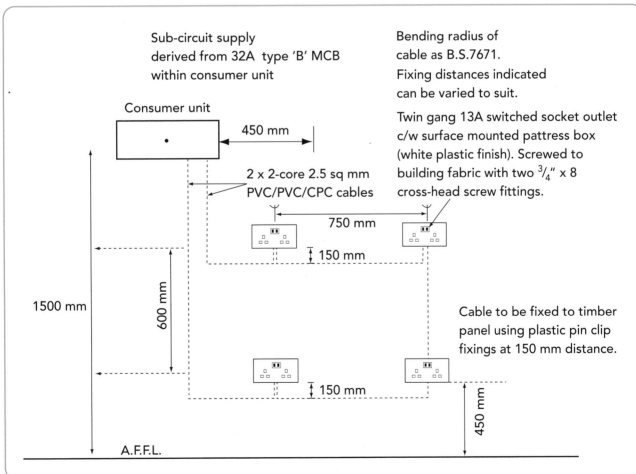

Sub-circuit supply derived from 32A type 'B' MCB within consumer unit

Bending radius of cable as B.S.7671. Fixing distances indicated can be varied to suit.

Twin gang 13A switched socket outlet c/w surface mounted pattress box (white plastic finish). Screwed to building fabric with two ³/₄" x 8 cross-head screw fittings.

Consumer unit

450 mm

2 x 2-core 2.5 sq mm PVC/PVC/CPC cables

750 mm

150 mm

Cable to be fixed to timber panel using plastic pin clip fixings at 150 mm distance.

1500 mm

600 mm

150 mm

450 mm

A.F.F.L.

Figure 10.6 Ring main sub-circuit.

> **Isolation** – the action taken to cut off power supply, preventing any person from accidentally making the power live again, potentially causing death.

Safe isolation

Safe **isolation** is of mandatory importance before any electrical work is undertaken on any circuit. The correct procedures to follow are as follows:

* Step 1 Identify sources of supply.
* Step 2 Isolate the supply.
* Step 3 Secure the isolation.
* Step 4 Test the equipment to ensure the system is dead.
* Step 5 Begin work on the circuit.

Step 1 – Identify

You must identify where the main source is operating from. This may not always be the obvious point, as you often find that work has been carried out on buildings over the years and power has been connected via different distribution boards or ring circuits. All the sources need to be identified and isolated prior to safe work taking place.

Step 2 – Isolate

Once the main source has been identified you can now isolate the supply. Simply switching off power breaks the current; however, isolation involves the cutting off of an already dead circuit, so that the re-closing of the switch will not make it live again.

Step 3 – Secure

To avoid and prevent any unauthorised re-closing of the contacts and making the circuit live, the isolator must be securely locked off. This is commonly done by putting a padlock on the system. The padlock key is kept with the person who is undertaking the task until the work has been carried out. The authorised key holder can then unlock the isolator and reconnect the power.

Step 4 – Test

A test must be carried out on the equipment to ensure that the equipment and system is dead. All tests must be done with good quality test equipment that is in good working condition. The equipment must have a certificate to prove it has passed a test and will give accurate readings. First, the voltage supply must be tested on a known unit prior to use. Then tests between the phase and neutral, phase and earth, and neutral and earth single-phase supplies are carried out. For three-phase supplies, test between:

* brown and black
* brown and grey
* grey and black
* brown and blue
* black and blue
* grey and blue and brown and green/yellow
* grey and green/yellow
* black and green/yellow
* blue and green/yellow.

You will still find old systems with the old colours of red and black for single-phase and red, yellow and blue for three-phase.

Step 5 – Begin work

Once the other four steps have been carried out you may begin the work. Some larger companies may operate a 'permit to work' system. This is a system designed for isolation purposes, and only allows authorised personnel to work on the designated piece of equipment. Danger signs should be put in place to notify others that there is an electrician working in that area.

case study

Carl is working in an occupied house and needs to carry out repairs to a lighting system. He has isolated the supply for the piece of equipment he needs to work on, but then is called away to another, more urgent, job. He leaves immediately and doesn't return to the job until the following day.

Questions and activities

1. What procedures should Carl have followed before he left the owner's premises?

2. What problems might Carl's action cause the occupier?

3. List the actions Carl should have taken when he isolated the supply.

Basic electrical tasks

TRY THIS

Install a lighting sub-circuit comprising four lighting points with one-way switch control (surface-mounted). Your installation should be in accordance with B.S.7671.

Procedure

1. Develop circuit and wiring diagrams for the circuit to be installed.

2. Using a spirit level and chalk, mark positions of all components and horizontal/vertical lines for all cable alignment.

3. Install electrical components to timber fabric in accordance with layout drawings as:

   * Lighting points comprising 2 x lighting pendants, 1 x batten lamp holder, 1 x bulkhead fitting. All these should be fixed at 300 mm centre to centre.

   * Lighting switches comprising 4 x 1-way surface-mounted switches directly below each lighting point, 450 mm centre to centre.

4. Lighting points to be secured using 2 (1 x 8) cross-head fixing screws.

5. Switch pattress boxes to be secured using 2 x (3/4 x 8) cross-head fixing screws, ensuring level alignment.

6. A two-core 1.5 mm^2 PVC/PVC/CPC cable derived from a 6 amp single-pole type B MCB within the consumer unit shall be installed to the first lighting point.

7. Cable shall be installed neatly and follow chalk lines. Clip at 150 mm spacing distance using approved cable clips.

8. Once all the cable is installed, PVC sheathing is removed, with care taken not to damage the PVC insulation.

   * Circuit protective conductors (CPC earth) to be identified using green/yellow sleeving and connected to the earthing terminal.

   * Components to be connected in accordance with your wiring diagram, ensuring that all of the connections are mechanically and electrically secure. The minimum amount of PVC insulation is to be removed to ensure that no copper conductor is exposed to touch.

   * All switch-wires to be identified using brown sleeving (unless twin brown cable is used).

   * Two-core 0.75 mm^2 white flexible cable is to be used from the ceiling rose to the lamp holder.

   * Cord grips to be used in each ceiling rose and lamp holder.

continues...

Testing

Before connecting to the mains supply, the current must be inspected and tested in accordance with B.S.7671 (part 7 section 712, B.S.7671).

1. Inspection shall cover the following:

   * connection of conductors

   * identification of conductors

   * routing of cables

   * connection of single-pole devices

   * connection of accessories and equipment

   * methods of protection against electric shock etc.

2. Testing (part 7 section 713 B.S.7671) shall comprise the following:

   * continuity of protective conductors

   * continuity of ring circuit conductors

   * insulation resistance (500 V)

   * polarity.

3. Upon satisfactory completion of inspection and testing, a functional test shall be performed in the presence of your teacher or tutor.

Your teacher or tutor can assess you on this task using the criteria marking sheet in the Appendices page 225.

EVIDENCE

Calculate how much it would cost for the material that you have just used for the *Try This* activity above.

* Twin and earth cable 6242Y	@£0.40p/metre
* 4 x 1-way switch	@£1.10p each
* 1 box of cable clips	@£2.52p each
* 2 x lighting pendants	@£2.15p each
* 1 x lamp batten holder	@£2.25 each
* 1 x black prismatic bulkhead fitting	@£5.95 each
* 4 m twin and earth cable 1.5 mm	@£0.40p/metre
* 2 x 16 mm depth 1-gang surface boxes	@£0.65p each
* 1 box 1 x 8 cross-head screws	@£1.50/box
* 1 box 3/4 x 8 cross-head screws	@£1.40/box
* 1 x consumer unit	@£74.50 each

All prices are to be inclusive of 17.5% VAT

TRY THIS

Ring main sub-circuit

In accordance with B.S.7671, install a ring main sub-circuit comprising 4 x 13 amp twin-gang switched socket outlets (surface-mounted).

Procedure

1. Develop circuit and wiring diagrams.

2. Using spirit level and chalk, mark positions of all components and horizontal/vertical lines for cable alignment.

3. Install 4 x twin-gang patress boxes (25 mm depth) to timber fabric using 2 x 3/4 x 8 cross-head fixing screws in accordance with dimensional drawing.

4. 2 x two-core 2.5 mm² PVC/PVC/CPC cables, derived from a 32 amp type B single-pole MCB within the consumer unit, shall be routed in accordance with the dimensional drawing.

5. Cables shall be installed neatly and follow chalk lines. Clip at 150 mm distance with appropriate cable clips.

6. Once all cables are installed, sheathing shall be removed, with care taken not to damage PVC insulation.

7. Circuit protective conductors (CPCs) to be identified using green/yellow sleeving and connected to the earthing terminal of the socket outlet plate.

8. Phase and neutral conductors to be connected to appropriate terminals of the socket outlet plate, ensuring all connections are mechanically and electrically secure, with no copper conductor exposed outside the terminals.

9. Each leg of the ring main shall be connected within the consumer unit. Phase/neutral/earth connections shall follow correct numbering and sequence. Sufficient cable length (cable slack) shall be allowed within consumer unit to ensure cable connections are free from stress/strain.

10. Before connecting to the mains supply, the current is to be inspected and tested in accordance with B.S.7671 (part 7 section 712, B.S.7671)

11. Inspection shall cover the following:

    * connection of conductors

    * identification of conductors

    * routing of cables

    * selection of conductors for current-carrying capacity

    * connection of single-pole devices

    * connection of accessories and equipment

continues...

* presence of fire barriers

* methods of protection against electric shock etc.

12. Testing (part 7 section 713 B.S.7671) shall comprise the following:

    * continuity of protective conductors

    * continuity of ring dual-circuit conductors

    * insulation resistance

    * polarity.

13. Upon satisfactory completion of inspection and testing, a functional test shall be performed in the presence of your teacher or tutor.

Your teacher or tutor can assess you on this task using the criteria marking sheet in the Appendices page 225.

Health, safety and welfare

In this section you will learn about...

* **health and safety regulations**

* **hazards associated with electricity.**

The Health, Safety and Welfare Regulations 1992 govern all workplaces and buildings that are not part of any domestic premises. These are the common places of work for people, and rules must be put in place to guide, protect and ensure adequate welfare for people whilst they are at work.

All work undertaken on site is the responsibility of the tradesman, therefore any mess made by the tradesman must be cleaned up periodically and not left to the last minute. Cables, pipes, fixtures and fittings create tripping hazards, and it is therefore of mandatory importance that they are adequately stacked, coiled or assembled to avoid any slips, trips and falls.

SAFE✝Y TIP

Before studying this section, look again at Unit 3: *Developing skills and working safely in construction.*

The following are required to be adequate in the working environment:

* heating
* lighting
* ventilation
* space
* cleanliness
* facilities to eat and drink
* drying facilities
* toilet facilities
* hot and cold running water supply
* access and **egress**.

Regulations

Accidents on site are commonly caused by faulty tools and equipment. All power tools should have a Portable Appliance Test (PAT) sticker on them. This proves that an electrical power tool which has an 110 V or 230 V output has been checked in accordance with the company procedures for leakages and damage. These power tools are also covered under the Provision and Use of Work Equipment Regulations 1998 (PUWER). These regulations cover any tools or equipment used by an employee on site. PUWER only covers on-site activities or work away from your home. It does not apply to domestic work undertaken in a private house.

Electrical accidents

Every year about 1000 accidents occur at work which involve electricity. The most common accidents are burns and electric shock. Around 40 of these are fatal. Electricity is all around us, but we cannot see or smell it. It can kill us, and the non-fatal shocks can trigger secondary actions that can lead to further injury. This may also cause falls from a height and other accidents.

All these accidents are generally caused by faulty devices, poor workmanship or negligence in the planning and implementation of installation.

Electrical hazards

Some of the main hazards when dealing with electrical equipment are:

* unqualified or unauthorised personnel working with electrical installations
* contact with live components
* working with electricity in wet conditions
* working with electrical components in a confined space
* electrical faults which could trigger a fire or explosion
* overloaded plug sockets
* failure to unwind electrical extension leads
* failure to carry out adequate safety checks prior to using electrical appliances.

All the previously mentioned hazards can be avoided if care and attention are maintained while using electrical appliances.

Safe working

Here are some tips for safe working:

* Try to reduce the voltage where you are working from 230 volts to 110 volts.

* Ensure all appliances are PAT tested.

* Only allow competently trained electricians to undertake work.

* Ensure all cables are adequately protected.

* Ensure all electrical tools and equipment are safe and in good working order.

* Choose the correct tool or piece of equipment for the specified job.

* Use the correct cable connectors to join two cables together, and do not use pieces of tape to cover bare wire.

* Check cables, switches and plugs are safe prior to use.

* Use an RCD breaker where possible to reduce electric shock.

* Switch off and unplug any appliances before you start working on them.

Be aware that all electrical components can cause serious damage to you no matter how small the part may be, so always take care and ask a fully trained, qualified and competent electrician to undertake any electrical repair to appliances or systems.

If you suspect something is wrong with a piece of equipment, do not use it, and label it for others to see.

Marking schemes

Basic woodworking joints marking schedule

Standards Required	Achieved Yes	Achieved No
Risk assessment complete and correct		
Workshop rod complete and accurate		
Cutting list complete and timber identified correctly		
Correct tools and PPE identified and requested		
No gaps exceeding 0.5mm		
Joints square		
Finished joints free from defects		
Joints dressed to good standard with no pencil lines showing		
Clean and tidy workstation maintained at all times		
Work safely carried out at all times		

Basic frame marking schedule

Standards Required	Achieved Yes	Achieved No
Risk assessment complete and correct		
Workshop rod complete and accurate		
Cutting list complete and timber identified correctly		
Correct tools and PPE identified and requested		
No gaps exceeding 0.5mm		
Frame square =/- 2mm		
Frame is same size as workshop rod +/- 2mm		
Finished joints free from defects		
Joints dressed to good standard with no pencil lines showing		
Clean and tidy workstation maintained at all times		
Work safely carried out at all times		

Electrical practical marking criteria sheet

		Yes	No
1.	Engineering information interpreted correctly		
2.	Measuring and marking out accurately produced		
3.	Accessories secured correctly		
4.	Cable clipped neatly and securely		
5.	Cable bend with acceptable radius		
6.	Sufficient spare at accessories		
7.	CPC correctly sleeved		
8.	Correct amount of sheathing removed		
9.	Conductor insulation undamaged		
10.	Terminations secure and conductor doubled where appropriate		
11.	Conductors identified		
12.	Cord grip used (if applicable)		
13.	Flex terminations secured		
14.	Correct fuse/neutral sequence in consumer unit		
15.	Inspection and testing correctly carried out		
16.	Functional testing correct		

Glossary

Abrade 183 – to scrape or wear away by rubbing.

Backnut 198 – a locking nut on the screwed shank of a tap, valve or pipe fitting for securing it to some other object.

Bats 154 – bricks cut along the stretcher face leaving the header intact.

Bevel 118 – a sloping edge.

Body language 75 – body movements, gestures and facial expressions.

Burr 196 – a rough edge or area left on material, after it has been cast, cut, or drilled.

Capillary attraction 204 – the process by which a liquid is drawn up the surface of a solid material.

Carpentry 14 – structural woodwork.

Chamfering 118 – bevelling a corner with an equal amount removed from each face.

Closers 154 – bricks that are cut along the header of a brick leaving the stretcher intact.

Contract of employment 30 – agreement between employer and employee.

Course 155 – a single row of brickwork.

Damp-proof course (DPC) 143 – a purpose-built, waterproof layer inserted into a wall to prevent rising damp from penetrating the building.

Deciduous 123 – trees that lose their leaves in winter.

Dermatitis 59 – inflammation of the skin caused by irritants.

Dovetail 114 – similar to a tenon but smaller and tapered.

Dry bond 155 – laying bricks without mortar with a gap of 10 mm between them along the first course of a wall.

Egress 222 – the exit or way out.

Evergreen 123 – trees that do not lose their leaves in winter.

Flag 172 – tip of a paint brush.

Gauge 143 – the correct brick or block height in a wall.

Global warming 100 – the rise in the overall temperature of the Earth's atmosphere and oceans.

Grain 114 – the natural texture within a piece of timber.

Greenhouse gases 100 – gases, such as methane and carbon dioxide whose increased presence in the atmosphere traps the sun's heat, causing global warming.

Half-brick walling 152 – the simplest brick walling. The wall is half a brick thick.

Hand board or **hawk** 170 – board with a handle underneath allowing it to be carried flat, on which to carry mixed filler, etc.

Hardwood 123 – wood from deciduous, broad leaved trees.

Header 155 – the end of a brick.

Heart 126 – the centre of a log.

Hierarchy of control 56 – a system of controls starting with the most effective control. If this is not possible, then move to the next control and so on.

Housing joint 127 – a joint with a slot in one piece of wood to house an equivalent shape in the joining piece of wood.

Incandescence 205 – glowing light created by heat.

Ingest 168 – take a substance into the stomach.

Ironmongery 112 – metal fitments to wooden structures, e.g. bolts.

ISO 9000 45 – set of standards for companies to work to.

Isolation 216 – cutting off power supply, preventing any person from accidentally making the power live again.

joinery 14 – small-scale wood construction.

Joint 155 – the gap between laid bricks, filled with mortar.

Laying off 172 – the last stroke of a brush over a wet paint surface.

Leaf 154 – layer of walling.

Length out 172 – the amount of visible filling in a paint brush.

Make good 183 – prepare a surface before work by filling holes, sanding down etc.

Marking off 113 – marking timber before cutting.

Masonry 140 – solid construction material such as bricks and stone.

Micro-bore 201 – copper pipe with diameter of 8 mm or 10 mm.

Miniature circuit breaker (MCB) 215 – an automatic switch that opens when too much current flows through the circuit, cutting off the electricity supply and preventing any damage to the circuit. The MCB is undamaged by the operation.

Mortar 140 – lime, cement, sand and water mix used to fix bricks and other masonry.

New build 166 – a newly constructed building.

Nibs 184 – fine particles on a surface.

Oxidisation 202 – a chemical reaction between a substance with oxygen, forming a new compound called an oxide.

Paring 115 – shaving down a piece of wood, until the correct size and shape is reached.

Partitions 112 – floor to ceiling wood-framed panels used to divide up space inside buildings.

PAYE 34 – Deductions from your salary for tax, National Insurance etc. before you receive it.

Perp 155 – perpendicular joint in bricklaying.

Personal audit 72 – assessment of one's strengths and weaknesses particularly in the work environment.

Personal statement 88 – brief statement by an individual about themselves as a person and a prospective employee.

Pile 171 – fibres cut and fixed to a surface.

Plant 57 – large machinery used on a construction site.

Plumb 141 – perpendicular.

Portfolio 88 – student's or trainee's evidence of work completed and job hunting undertaken.

Posture 75 – the alignment of your body when you stand, sit and walk.

Potable water 202 – water which is fit for humans to drink.

PPE 37 – personal protective equipment, such as a hard hat or goggles, that must be worn when undertaking certain tasks to protect the worker.

Putty 170 – an oil-based filler that sets very hard. Used to fix glass into windows.

Quoin 155 – corner of a wall.

Recovery position 67 – position a casualty is put into following an accident or injury to aid recovery.

Recycle 96 – to use materials again, either for a different use from their original one, or by adapting or modifying the material.

Residence 166 – property where someone lives.

Residual current device (RCD) 215 – a device that monitors the current flowing in phase and neutral conductors and cuts off supply if an earth fault occurs.

Resinous 123 – containing resin – a strong-smelling, sticky substance in the wood.

Résumé 89 – a C.V.

Reuse 96 – to use second-hand materials again without modifying them.

Rhinitis 59 – inflammation of the nasal passages causing a runny nose.

Salary 33 – yearly earnings paid in equal monthly parts.

Season 124 – the controlled drying of green timber before it is used.

Softwood 123 – wood from trees with narrow leaves that are usually evergreen.

Staff handbook 31 – information, about your workplace provided by your employer.

Stretcher 155 – the long side of a brick.

Synthetic 171 – something manufactured rather than produced naturally.

Temper 201 – the degree of hardness in a metal.

Tenon 114 – a projecting piece of wood made to fit into a corresponding cavity to form a joint.

Terms and conditions 30 – details of your employment.

Timber 112 – wood prepared for carpentry or joinery.

Toolkit 30 – in this context, guideline documents to help companies develop and maintain good working relationships with their employees.

Toxic 168 – poisonous.

Trowel occupations 12 – bricklaying and plastering.

Union nut 198 – a screwed pipe fitting, usually brass or low carbon steel.

Wages 33 – earnings paid daily, weekly or fortnightly, based on hours worked in the period or work done.

Walling to a line 155 – filling in walling between two corners.

Well graded 157 – sand that has small, medium and large particles in it.

Wood occupations 12 – carpentry and joinery.

Index

Note: a 'g' following the page number shows that there is a glossary definition.